CUSHLA AND HER BOOKS

DATE DUE

DEMCO, INC. 38-2931

CUSHLA
AND HER BOOKS

Dorothy Butler

THE HORN BOOK, INC.
BOSTON

This book is based on *Cushla: a Case Study – Three Years of Enrich-ment in the Life of a Handicapped Child*, an original investigation presented for the Diploma in Education, the University of Auckland, New Zealand, 1975.

Copyright © 1975 and 1979 by Dorothy Butler
First British edition 1979
First American edition 1980

All rights reserved. No part of this book may be reproduced or utilized in any form or by any means, electronic or mechanical, including photocopying, recording or by an infor-mation storage and retrieval system, without permission in writing from the publisher. Inquiries should be addressed to The Horn Book, Inc., Park Square Building, 31 St James Avenue, Boston, Massachusetts 02116.

Library of Congress Cataloging in Publication Data
Butler, Dorothy, 1925–
  Cushla and her books.
  "Based on Cushla: a case study – three years of enrichment in the life of a handicapped child, original investigation presented for the Diploma in Education, the University of Auckland, New Zealand, 1975."
  Bibliography:
  Includes index.
  1. Books and reading for children – New Zealand – Case studies. 2. Handicapped children – Education (Preschool) – New Zealand – Case studies. 3. Yeoman, Cushla, 1971–   4. Developmentally disabled children – New Zealand – Biography. I. Title
Z1037.A1B89   1980   028.5   79–25695   ISBN 0–87675–279–2   ISBN 0–87675–283–0 (pbk.)

Printed in Great Britain
The permissions acknowledged on pages 5 and 6 constitute an extension of this copyright page.

Acknowledgments

This book was made possible by the efforts of Patricia Yeoman, Cushla's mother, who faithfully and efficiently documented her daughter's development from birth. My gratitude goes also to her husband, Stephen, for his consideration and support, and to Johannes Everts of the Education Department, University of Auckland, whose encouragement, and insistence on precision, were important factors in the production of the original thesis.

To Elaine Moss and Nancy Chambers, whose joint enthusiasm led to the appearance of a shortened form of the thesis in *Signal 22*, my affection and gratitude.

D. B.

Grateful acknowledgment is also made to the following authors, artists, agents, and publishers for their kind permission to use text and illustrations:

Plate I Illustration by Dick Bruna from *B is for Bear*. Copyright © 1967 by C. Mercis b.v. Reprinted by permission of the publisher.

Plate II Illustration by Rodney Peppé from *The House that Jack Built*. Copyright © 1970 by Rodney Peppé. Used by permission of Delacorte Press.

Plate III Illustration by Thomas and Wanda Zacharias from *Where Is the Green Parrot?* Copyright © 1969 by Thomas and Wanda Zacharias. Used with permission of Delacorte Press/Seymour Lawrence.

Plate IV Illustration by Lois Lenski from *Papa Small*. Copyright 1951 by Lois Lenski. Reprinted by permission of the David McKay Company, Inc.

Plate V Illustration by Margaret Bloy Graham from *Harry the Dirty Dog* by Gene Zion. Pictures copyright © 1956 by Margaret Bloy Graham. By permission of Harper & Row Publishers, Inc.

Plate VI Illustration by Frank Francis from *Grandmother Lucy and Her Hats* by Joyce Wood, illustrated by Frank Francis. Copyright © 1968 by Joyce Wood. Used by permission of Collins Publishers, London.

To the memory of Val

Introduction

Cushla's story is a remarkable piece of work, both in content and in the method of presentation. It is an in-depth study of how a highly original book-based compensatory programme was provided for a child with developmental handicaps. The family applied the best information they could get on child development to Cushla's particular problems with insight, drive and determination.

Some years ago I advised Dorothy Butler not to make this study of her granddaughter. It seemed to be too personal an account to be reduced to the academic task of presenting a dissertation for a Diploma in Education. I had worked with the parents of many children who needed help in growing up. I was overprotective of Cushla's family and of Cushla's own reactions. Perhaps, as an adult, she would not read this account of her own early years with favour. Undoubtedly I was wrong about her family. Her intelligent, persistent parents made so many strong and caring decisions against the tide of professional opinion in her early years. These are apparent in the text. And they were backed by an unusually supportive extended family who provided extra resources for these young parents raising a first child who had perplexing handicaps.

Cushla's story demonstrates the ingenuity of parents casting around for ways to soothe a wakeful, sick child. They even read children's books to her from the age of four months more to fill the long hours of carrying her around than in a deliberate attempt to reach her understanding. It so happened that one of the resources of the extended family was a love of children's books and an encyclopaedic knowledge about them. So Cushla had an extraordinary, and very early, introduction to the world of books.

9

Cushla and her books

From time to time voices are raised about the problems of handicapped children. But seldom with the positive implications of this story. Hard work, intelligent action, affectionate persistence, a healthy, positive but realistic appraisal of a series of perplexing situations led this family past the negative predictions of some experts until by three years of age it was apparent that Cushla, a puzzlingly exceptional child in so many respects, was surpassing many normal children in some of the things she could do. This book does not provide a recipe which all parents could follow diligently with similar dividends for all handicapped children, but it does contain creative ideas.

I think that many parents of pre-school children will find in this book a story of the enrichment that comes from parental care and a wealth of shared experiences. And they will learn so much about children's books – of the range available – both old and new; the interweaving of book experiences with real everyday ones; the delights of shared knowledge and creative fantasy; books as a springboard to further learning in a broad sense.

Credit must go to the teller of the tale who knew the people so well, and loved the books they shared, who stood back from the intimacy to be objective, and who caught so sensitively in her writing the things that mattered most to Cushla as she learned how to learn.

Marie Clay,
Professor of Education,
University of Auckland, New Zealand

Contents

List of Illustrations

Chapter One

BIRTH TO SIX MONTHS

Cushla was born on the 18th December, 1971, at 2.40 in the morning. Her mother, Patricia, was aged twenty years, five months and her father, Stephen, exactly one year older. Cushla's father was present at her birth, and had been with his wife throughout her labour. The baby weighed 6 lbs 9 oz.

The pregnancy had been a normal one, the mother sitting and passing examinations towards a Bachelor of Science degree in October and November immediately prior to the birth. The couple had met and married while at university.

Contact was made early in the pregnancy with the North Shore Parents' Centre, the prospective parents subsequently playing an active part in a newly-formed group in Devonport. This seaside suburb of Auckland, New Zealand, is a mixture of the old and the new. Many students and young couples struggling to make their way occupy flats in old, two-storeyed timber houses which were once gracious family homes.

Cushla's only immediately apparent defect was the presence of an extra digit on each hand. This consisted of a perfectly-formed but jointless extra finger attached (between the two joints) to the little finger.

The parents gave permission to remove these, and they were immediately 'tied off' with twine, so that they withered and fell off within a few days. Cushla's mother protested at this method, and was upset that the baby screamed while it was being carried out. She was assured that it was painless for the baby, but saw no reason to believe this.

Cushla was heavily jaundiced as a result of an encephalo-haematoma, discernible as a large swelling on her head. The jaundice is caused by the excessive flow of waste matter into the blood as the swelling breaks down.

The parents were assured that this process would shortly be completed, and that the blood condition would then return to normal.

When, after two days, this had not happened and, in fact, the extent of the jaundice had increased, both baby and mother were transferred to the National Women's Hospital and treatment for the jaundice commenced. This consisted of exposure to a 'cold light' procedure which had recently been introduced.

It was by now apparent to Cushla's parents that all was far from well. There had been feeding difficulties since birth, despite a plentiful breast-milk supply, and the hospital was clearly concerned about the baby's uneven, rasping breathing. Both parents knew that a high level of jaundice could lead to impairment of the brain cells, and the baby's almost continuous crying served only to intensify their anxiety. They were assured by the hospital that a constant check was being kept on the jaundice level, and that, if it reached a certain critical point, a changeover of blood would be effected. This point was not reached; the level began to decline, and it was hoped that all would now be well.

Cushla was seven days old on Christmas morning 1971, when her parents were told that they might take her home.

This they did with great joy. The baby's condition had so far engendered considerable apprehension in both their minds, but they were confident that her troubles were behind her, and that time and care would produce the healthy baby that seemed their right.

At home, their hopes were unrealised. The baby was constantly distressed, and often screamed until she was blue. Her breathing difficulties increased, and she hardly slept. Feeding her adequately seemed impossible, and she needed constant attention, day and night.

Before long, they had become anxious regarding her ability to see and hear. Cushla seemed cut off from the rest of the world and, at a time when the normal baby is starting to focus on faces as they come

16

within his range, she seemed unaware of the presence of other people.

Reassuringly, she began to respond with a smile at six weeks, if care was taken to allow her time to focus at close quarters, and shortly afterwards it became apparent that she could see brightly coloured objects if they were held close enough to her face.

At about two months it was first noticed that Cushla was apt, on occasion, to jerk convulsively. At the time, little attention was paid to this tendency; it might always have been caused by a noise, or other stimulus, and did not occur in any pattern. Meanwhile, more cause for concern attached to the baby's failure to gain weight satisfactorily, and the onset of almost constant ear and throat infection. Frequent visits to the doctor were necessary and it was in due course suggested that specialist help was needed. An appointment was made at the Auckland Hospital by the doctor attending Cushla; they would see the baby in three months' time.

Long before the day for this appointment arrived, Cushla's parents and grandparents were so alarmed by the baby's condition that they decided to consult a specialist privately. Irritating skin rashes on both face and body had been added to the baby's afflictions, and immediate attention seemed essential.

Accordingly, the hospital appointment was cancelled, and a paediatrician consulted.

His diagnosis was as follows: Cushla had a small hole in the heart, and was suffering from an asthmatic condition which was linked to her eczematous skin rash. He noted also that she had very small nasal passages which impaired her breathing, and drew the parents' attention to her exceptionally high interior mouth cavity and the unusually low setting of her ears on her head.

A return appointment was made, and prescriptions given for the asthma and eczema. Anxiety, if anything, was increased, and the eternal round of caring for the ailing, fractious baby continued.

By three months, Cushla was well behind the normal baby in most aspects of her development. Her lack of arm control was marked; her arms seemed to swing involuntarily out and back from her body. She did not attempt to pick up any object. It was noted, however, that if she was placed in her cot in such a way that her arms were fixed in front of her, she could direct a hand towards a toy that was hanging on the side of the cot. She could not hold her head up, and could not focus her eyes except briefly on an object held close to her face; she was unable to tolerate outside light, even on a dull day. Despite almost constant antibiotic treatment, the ear and throat infections persisted.

As several more months passed, no improvement occurred, and the baby accordingly fell further behind normal standards. Physically, she lacked co-ordination and vigour; she did not 'cling' as does a normal baby, and her back and legs seemed 'floppy'. Her jerking reactions had increased to a point at which they were clearly abnormal.

The young parents, faced with this situation, were already embarked upon a course of support which they have pursued, in principle, ever since.

Cushla was held closely at all times unless actually asleep. She was never left to cry alone. Being held was not always sufficient to comfort her, but was practised nonetheless. Her spells of lying on the floor or in her pram were confined to those times when she seemed able, with adult help, to 'play'. Her hands would be directed to, and placed on, brightly-coloured toys which were hung within reach, and she was helped to 'feel' these with her mouth.

Books were introduced for the first time at four months, when it was realised that Cushla could see clearly only if an object was held close to her face. Filling in the long hours during the day and night necessitated some parental ingenuity, and desperation certainly played a part. The baby would look at a book; she constituted a totally captive audience, and reading the text gave her mother something constructive to do. Cushla's mother turned to books naturally, at this time, for help.

Surprisingly, Cushla's legs seemed to develop in strength and co-ordination after nine weeks and she made strenuous efforts, if placed on her stomach, to roll over. This was encouraged by her mother, who tried to 'show' Cushla, by swinging the baby's legs and hips backwards and over, that she could roll

18

over. At five months, Cushla accomplished the feat alone; a considerable achievement, as her arms could not be used for leverage, and her face remained in contact with the mat until the sudden 'flip' was achieved.

At this time, Cushla's parents bought and experimented with a haversack-type carrier, in the hope that it might help Cushla to see things about her, and encourage her to use her arms. It was quite unsuccessful; the baby clearly needed the constant support of adult arms, and the attempt was abandoned.

This, then, was the stage Cushla had reached by the age of six months, when her condition suddenly deteriorated.

Cushla was admitted to the Auckland Hospital on 24th June, 1972, with suspected meningitis.

A lumbar puncture was performed and the results were negative. The baby, although very ill, had not contracted meningitis.

Her immediate condition was traced to a urinary infection, and, in the course of exhaustive tests, hydronephrosis of the left kidney was revealed. This is a condition in which the kidney, whatever its actual condition, cannot function because the funnel-shaped outlet is misshapen and blocked. In Cushla's case, the area was swollen to 'massive proportions' and even an X-ray could not reveal the condition of the kidney.

Even if originally normal, the kidney is in increasing danger of damage in this condition. In Cushla's case, the necessary operation was out of the question at this time, because of her generally frail state. The findings of the specialist who had seen Cushla at three and a half months were confirmed, although there was no evidence of asthma at this stage. In addition, Cushla's spleen was revealed by X-ray as misshapen and enlarged, and an electro-encephalogram showed an abnormal brain impulse pattern.

Cushla was six months old. Her short life had so far occasioned her parents a degree of fear and anxiety that would have been unimaginable to either of them before her birth. She was to remain in hospital for ten weeks.

As the days and then weeks passed, the outlook was bleak, and did not improve. Cushla's parents gradually came to see that, for their child, there was to be no 'cure'.

Mental retardation was constantly mentioned as the baby failed to use her hands or react in normal ways to the world about her. Even when unspoken, the assumption was clearly present in the minds of doctors and nurses. Cushla's mother, during this time, borrowed books from the library on 'the handicapped child' in preparation for what lay ahead. Even here, only doubt existed; the baby's future was totally unknowable.

Chapter Two

EIGHT TO NINE MONTHS

At thirty-five weeks, Cushla had just been discharged from hospital, after a ten-week-long stay. Her genetic defect had not as yet been discovered; the current diagnosis was of a brain disease which, if not controlled, would lead to progressive mental deterioration.

Electro-encephalograms taken while Cushla was in hospital had revealed an unusual brain impulse pattern; a tendency to convulsive jerking (earlier noted) had intensified, and it was thought to be essential to control this reaction. Accordingly the drug Prednizone had been prescribed and its use begun two weeks before her discharge. Her parents had been warned that the drug would lower her bodily resistance to infection, but that its use was imperative. An obvious and immediate effect was the swelling of her face and limbs. A deceptive look of health replaced Cushla's former frail appearance, though closer inspection revealed a soft fleshiness.

The baby's mother had undertaken to chart her 'jerks' during certain periods each day. This, plus the additional requirement that she record details of bowel and bladder output had been a condition of discharge.

The parents were informed at this time that Cushla's kidney condition (hydronephrosis of the left kidney) required removal or repair, but that the baby's physical condition was too precarious to allow this. Cushla's mother recalls this period as one of the lowest in terms of hope for the baby's future.

When she was thirty-five weeks old, Cushla was tested in her own home. The Gesell Developmental Schedule was administered by a psychologist from the University of Auckland.

This schedule consists of a series of tests designed to show a child's development, in different areas, as compared with that of a normal, or average, child of the same age.

On the 'personal-social' test, Cushla was placed at a typical twenty-four-week level, as against her actual age of thirty-five weeks.

This score includes both level of response to other people, and competence in meeting the child's own, personal needs. Clearly, Cushla's score derives more from the former than the latter of these.

The normal child of this age smiles at his own reflection in a mirror, responds to another person's smiling face and is inclined to be more shy with strangers than with members of his immediate family – an indication that he is starting to discriminate. Cushla exhibited all these responses provided care was taken to help her achieve focus. She was, however, fairly indiscriminately responsive to other people.

The other parts of the personal-social test were quite beyond Cushla. Whereas a normal baby of thirty-five weeks can hold and drink from a bottle and accept, and feed itself with, a biscuit (chewing, not sucking while eating) Cushla could not use her hands at all, and characteristically seemed unable to cope with food when it was placed in her mouth.

The psychologist's report noted that 'C's arm movements occurred involuntarily, her arms swinging in an unusual backward direction', and this disability certainly affected this score.

Even more did it affect her 'adaptive' score, based on her ability at 'fine hand motor tasks, guided by eyes'. In this sphere, there was no achievement at all. (It is interesting to speculate on Cushla's possible performance on these tests if her hands and arms *had* been available to her. The fact of her focus difficulties might still have been expected to mar her performance; she was actually doubly handi-capped.) The normal child of eight months can, of course, pick up small objects with finger and thumb, manipulate toys roughly, crumple paper and shake a rattle purposefully.

In the field of gross motor abilities, Cushla's score of 'twenty-eight-week level on leg action' is in strict contrast to her 'nil' score on arm performance. (The report noted that, when Cushla was lying down, her arms 'tended to be at right angles, and remained that way' – also that, when sitting, she 'needed support, leaned forward, and did not use hands for support'.

By contrast, the normal child at thirty-five weeks sits without support, pulls himself up to a standing position with the help of available furniture, and crawls or moves three feet or more without assistance.

In the language field, Cushla was placed at the thirty-two-weeks level, only three weeks below that expected of a normal child. She responded to her own name, combined (unintelligible) syllables and was heard to copy sounds from her surroundings.

The Gesell test revealed Cushla's considerable degree of physical retardation.

It is significant, however, that before hospitalisation at the age of five and a half months, she had mastered the skill of rolling over, despite the near-uselessness of her arms. This was accomplished by a hip and leg throwing technique which, at that stage, seemed to demonstrate the beginning of a compensatory method. This ability had been lost during her time in hospital, despite her mother's attempts to help her re-learn it in the last few weeks of her stay.

It is also of note that Cushla's language was not significantly below normal at thirty-five weeks. It is likely that this score relates directly to the family's support of the baby during her weeks in hospital, and to the amount of verbal attention she was given – talking, singing, reading of picture books.

During the length of her stay, her mother would arrive at about 8 a.m. and stay with Cushla until her father's arrival at about 5 p.m. They would both then stay until 8 p.m. A member of the mother's family would come in each day at about noon to free her for a few hours.

Both Cushla's parents became convinced, after this experience, that their absence during the night had been seriously detrimental to her progress. She was always in a distressed condition when her mother arrived in the morning, and had certainly spent many hours awake and crying in the night.

Quite apart from the emotional effects of her distress, there was the physical consideration of her unsatisfactory respiration, and the harmful effect of long and distressed crying.

Cushla's regression during hospitalisation, and her extremely disturbed state upon discharge, led her parents to decide that they would never again leave her alone overnight in hospital. They have adhered firmly to this course, and the Auckland Hospital (at first, reluctantly) has co-operated with them and made provision for one or other of them to sleep in Cushla's room.

In the fields of personal-social and language development, Cushla's retardation at this stage was less marked (twenty-four weeks for personal-social, and thirty-two weeks for language). The most handicapping feature in her social development was probably her difficulty in focusing. If approached by a face, she would peer searchingly and then, quite suddenly, smile radiantly. There seemed to be more than just a friendly reaction in her smile; there was an element of discovery, as if a strenuous visual effort had been suddenly rewarded, as, indeed, it had. When the face was withdrawn beyond her field of vision (approximately eighteen inches), she would assume her usual expression of remoteness, perhaps better described as puzzled anxiety; it contained nothing of resignation or serenity.

The same factor seemed to govern her reaction to her own face in the mirror. She would first peer, and then focus, indicating clearly at that stage that she could now see her own image.

Although Cushla's vocalisation score was three weeks behind that of a normal baby at this stage, her mother recorded her impression that she 'sounded and responded vocally like any other baby of her age'.

Cushla required constant attention. She slept for short periods of time only; no longer than one half-hour, several times daily, and approximately two-hour stretches during the night. Between these night periods, she would often be awake for three to four hours at a time, usually unhappy and often very distressed.

During the day, Cushla's mother kept her with her at all times. A small wooden folding cot with dowelled sides and six-inch-high legs

24

was kept in the living room. It was thought that this cot would allow her less restricted vision than a pram, and provide a firmer surface for physical experimentation. As she was prone to fall asleep, when she did, very suddenly, and could never be 'tucked down to sleep' as could most normal babies, this proved a practical arrangement.

At other times, Cushla would lie on a rug on the floor. However, this proved less satisfactory than the cot; her attempts to reach toys invariably knocked them out of both her physical reach and her visual range.

Coloured toys were hung on a line stretched between the sides of her cot and this seemed the only way of ensuring that they stayed within her range. Even so, her physical resources were so limited at this time that she could not have experienced her surroundings in any way had she not had almost constant help. A practice was established of helping Cushla to grasp an object by closing her hands around it, supporting both the object and the baby's hands, and holding them to her mouth so that she could 'feel' them orally, as a normal baby does.

When obliged to go into another room, Cushla's mother invariably carried the baby with her unless she was asleep. Household tasks which could not be performed within the restrictions of Cushla's programme were left until the evening, when her father was at home and could help with either baby or chores.

The parents experimented again at this time with a 'baby pack' designed for carrying a baby on an adult back. Again it was unsuccessful; Cushla invariably slumped into an uncomfortable position and seemed 'out of touch'. She seemed to need the support and direction of adult arms if she was to see and experience the world at all.

By the same token, pram-riding was totally unsuccessful. The bouncing motion of the pram invariably resulted in the baby's assuming an uncomfortable position, and, again, she seemed quite unable to experience her surroundings. The overall impression one had of Cushla was that she was 'cut-off' from the world if denied close physical contact.

A practice developed at this time of carrying the baby around both inside and out and directing her attention to objects of interest – leaves, flowers, etc, outside, and pictures, ornaments, mirrors etc inside. It was at this stage that Cushla was first seen to be strongly attracted to specific objects. If carried into a room she would strain towards a part of the room in which, for example, a certain picture was hung. On being carried to the spot, she would, after focusing, show signs of recognition and excitement. (Her characteristic method of focusing at this time was to shake her head rapidly, blinking repeatedly until focus was achieved.)

Her concentration on her 'favourite' subjects for scrutiny was intense. In her grandmother's house, for example, a calendar hanging in the kitchen fascinated her. She would indicate her wish to look at it by leaning in its direction; on being held close she would make a strenuous effort to focus on the large black numbers underneath the coloured picture. She would then appear to 'scan' them, the whole procedure occupying several minutes. (It is worth emphasising that Cushla preferred the numbers here to the picture; this fascination with symbols will appear again in connection with picture books.)

Another of her favourite objects in her grandmother's house was a large, original black-and-white drawing of a Maori woman's head. As this picture was hung on the far side of a wide occasional table, one of Cushla's strong young adolescent uncles was often pressed into service to hold her at arm's length for the required length of viewing time!

It should be noted that Cushla's parents did have some help with this extending programme. Her mother's sister was at this stage in her second year at university, and came to live with the family when Cushla was a young baby. In common with other family members, this young aunt was prepared to observe the necessary conditions of constant care and attention to the baby, and was often able to relieve her sister for short periods.

It was not to be wondered at that Cushla came to know, and love, an extended circle of relatives, all of whom recognised her need for special attention, and loved her deeply in return.

It was at this stage, immediately after discharge from her ten-week-long stay in hospital, that the habit of using picture books with Cushla came to occupy a considerable proportion of her waking hours.

Two factors interacted in consolidating the practice. One was the recognised need to give the baby constant attention if she were to experience her surroundings at all. The other was, undoubtedly, the success achieved in interesting the baby in books.

Cushla's mother came from a family in which reading to children was an everyday occurrence, not confined to bedtime. It was natural, therefore, that books should be used as 'time-fillers'. Nine months was not thought to be too young for regular book use.

Moreover, Cushla was unable to occupy her time and attention in normal ways – crawling, pulling herself up, exploring objects encountered, tasting and watching everyday activities. Without one-to-one help, it is likely that she would have relapsed into a state of almost total non-involvement.

During reading sessions, Cushla would be held on an adult knee, her back supported by the front of the adult's body, and the book to be read held at an optimum distance from her eyes (this was established by observing her focusing technique).

Books were always 'read' from beginning to end, each page in turn being held close to the baby's eyes. As with the calendar, Cushla would use a scanning motion, often pausing to stare fixedly at a certain part of a picture.

B is for Bear by Dick Bruna is an alphabet book in which each left-hand page (white) contains one lower-case letter in large black print, in the lower left-hand corner. The right-hand page contains one simplified picture of an object (for example, a duck, a fish, an umbrella) in bright, primary colours, against a contrasting background. Cushla formed a strong attachment to this book. The single letter on each left-hand page obviously fascinated her, and she would gaze intently at it, then moving her eyes with great deliberation over to the picture on the opposite page. *A Story to Tell* by the same author was also popular, but has both left and right pages devoted to a simple picture. In this case there is no text, but a simple story implicit in the illustrations. *I Can Count* reverts to the plan used in *B is for Bear*, numbers being substituted for letters.

When showing Cushla one of these textless books, the adult would point in turn to objects pictured. Cushla learned to follow the adult finger with her eyes, but refused often to move to the next object if she wished to continue staring at something that interested her. She never smiled at what she saw; her expression was invariably one of intense concentration.

To the jingly-rhyme type of book she reacted differently. The rhythmic, rhyming text of *The Owl and the Pussycat* and the repetitive, ongoing flow of *The House that Jack Built* seemed to be soothing to her – particularly as the officiating adult was inclined to move in time to the rhythm. These poems and other nursery rhymes and songs were frequently repeated or sung to Cushla without the books, for example, when travelling in the car.

From this age onwards, Cushla always gave signs of recognising poems or songs; she would assume an expression of focused attention, and often smile and kick her legs with a jerking motion.

The Box with Red Wheels was Cushla's first favourite among the stories proper. It is unlikely that she understood the storyline, but she listened intently throughout, always, again, examining the pictures minutely. This book has, in common with *In the Busy Town* and *Beside the Busy Sea*, a quite remarkable clarity of form in its illustrations. The subjects (mainly farmyard animals) are clearly and colourfully depicted, and each page is framed in a red, decorated border.

Every book on the list in Appendix B was used successfully with the baby at this stage; that is, she would demonstrate the behaviour already described, unless too ill or distressed to be interested at all. However, the books specifically mentioned above were clearly superior in impact; increasingly, Cushla showed signs of excited recognition, waving her arms and kicking her legs when a favourite appeared. (It should not be thought that this was a vigorous response; Cushla was a frail child at this stage, and both her arm and leg movements were weak.)

Each of these books was read hundreds of times. Cushla's erratic sleeping pattern meant that it was often necessary to occupy her for long periods during the night.

The size of the book seemed immaterial at this time, although it is commonly recognised that very young children handle small books more successfully than large. This point had no relevance for Cushla; she could still not use her arms or hands at all.

Cushla's mother says that reading to the baby sprang as much from her desperation as from any initial certainty that it would help. Success led to perseverance; but certainly, the need to fill in the long hours, for both mother and baby, was a factor.

It should be added that music was also used, but that it never occupied her whole attention in the way books did. Her mother would play records, or sing, and dance with the baby, and she appeared to enjoy this, and would often laugh aloud. However, these were short periods; Cushla was hard to hold, and she was often ill. Reading was always possible, and books became entrenched as one of her links with the world.

This period emerges in retrospect as one in which Cushla's parents faced the reality of her handicaps, at the same time accepting their unknown nature and extent. The compensatory programme introduced at this time sprang partly from their expressed determination to 'keep her in touch', and partly from the need to fill in the hours that must be devoted to her care.

Cushla's inability to occupy herself in ways available to the normal baby probably increased her attentiveness to the books which were shown and read to her. One can only assume that the comfort and security of being constantly held and talked to helped to relieve the loneliness and fear that must afflict the child who is cut off from normal routes of communication. And so much is learned in the first year of life through the very senses of which Cushla was deprived: adequate sight, and manual and oral touch.

Whatever its reason of origin, the programme was established firmly at this time. And it was a two-way process; Cushla and her parents *were* in touch.

Chapter Three

NINE TO EIGHTEEN MONTHS

No marked improvement in Cushla's health took place during this period, but, very slowly, she began to progress physically.

At ten months she learned again to turn from her back to her stomach on the floor. As noted in the last chapter, this skill had been mastered at six months, but lost during her time in hospital.

At exactly twelve months, by which time Cushla could sustain short periods in a high chair, she learned to pick up a light object from the tray of the chair and carry it to her mouth. It was inevitably dropped, however, before she could place it in her mouth. By the same age, she could take her weight on her legs for a brief time and stand upright, if her hands were held. She could also sit alone for short periods if watched carefully, a stage achieved by the average child at approximately eight months.

Between eleven and twelve months, Cushla's 'jerking' reaction decreased, and finally disappeared. The drug Prednizone, which had been prescribed at seven months, was gradually reduced in dose and abandoned entirely at twelve months. The jerking has not recurred, although a tendency to 'twitchiness' has been noted in subsequent illnesses, when she has had a high temperature. This is characterised by a tendency for the face to twitch convulsively, while the limbs evince an irregular shivering reaction. The earlier jerking, by contrast, involved the whole body in a sudden sharp spasm.

Investigation of the kidney and spleen abnormalities continued, with barium X-rays becoming a regular feature of the painful and often frightening procedures to which the baby was subjected. During this whole period, Cushla suffered almost constantly from either an ear or a throat infection, or both simultaneously. Regular fortnightly visits were made to the Auckland Hospital, and the services of the family doctor constantly invoked. Her sleeping habits were still irregular in the extreme; broken nights and constant vigil were a feature of her parents' lives. Valium and other sedatives were prescribed and tried, but inevitably abandoned. Their effect was always to reduce Cushla's alertness during her waking hours, and her parents were almost fiercely determined that she should make the most of her faculties.

When Cushla was one year old, her mother and several other young women who had formed a group within the Parents' Centre movement before their babies' births decided to form a playgroup, meeting once weekly. Several families had children in the two-to-four years age group who were unable to gain admission to local pre-schools, and the group was seen as a compensatory or interim measure. Cushla's mother played a leading role in the establishment of this group, which provided the baby with the opportunity to watch other children playing and her mother with the companionship and help that she so badly needed at this time.

By fifteen months it was clear that Cushla's legs were strong enough to allow her to crawl, but that her arms were preventing mastery of the skill.

Her parents attempted a teaching programme at this stage, one of them supporting the baby's back from above so that her arms and legs were correctly positioned for crawling, the other moving the baby's hands for her as the supporting adult moved her forward. (It was clear that her legs were adequately developed for crawling; she would move her knees forward, in the appropriate manner, during this procedure.)

Two features convinced the parents that the programme could not succeed, at least at this stage. First, was the baby's muscular inability to take her weight on her arms, and, second, her lack of control over her arms. There was, so far, no indication at all that Cushla could have co-ordinated hand and knee movements and learned to crawl, even given adequate arm strength.

Nonetheless, she achieved a form of crawling. Supporting herself on her forearms on the floor, she would take several crawling 'steps'

31

with her knees, her arms remaining immobile. She would then push her arms forward, in a sliding movement, and repeat the process. In this way, she did move a few yards, although the process required too much effort for her to achieve any real mobility. (A further stage was achieved eight months later, at one year eleven months, by which time Cushla was taking a few steps alone. Still trying to crawl, she would move alternate arm and leg in the natural way, but using her left forearm instead of hand, and her right hand with arm extended. This allowed her to take most of her body weight on her left forearm. At no stage did she use *both* forearms for this process, and always her left.)

Meanwhile, practice was being given each day in walking, and Cushla responded with her usual spirit. Although quite lacking in balance, she would move her legs and try to walk if her hands were held, and by seventeen months she could walk a few steps with an adult holding one hand only. Pulling herself up, or 'walking round the furniture' was still impossible; her arms were neither strong enough nor co-ordinated enough to help with such an accomplishment. But her arms were, gradually, coming more under her control. Although at times (and certainly when her body was 'at rest' as against being involved in some activity) Cushla's arms would still swing out and backwards from her body, increasingly, she was bringing one or both arms forward and attempting to use her hands. By twelve months she was trying to turn the page of a book being read to her and by fifteen months she was able to do this with some skill. Pointing to objects in the pictures also became a feature of her book-handling at this time.

However, Cushla was eighteen months old before she could clap her hands; the effort to co-ordinate both arms was difficult for her, and only achieved after months of coaching and apparent failure. Once she had mastered the art, she became a furious clapper! And this was no delicate hand-clapping; with arms extended at right-angles to her body, Cushla would assume an air of extreme concentration, her eyes blinking furiously and her mouth held in the slightly open, rigidly set attitude which always denoted the onset of intense effort. Then she would swing her arms inward and together, and at the

32

moment of impact, the rigid expression would turn to one of startled delight.

Cushla's satisfaction was equalled only by her parents' joy at her accomplishment.

The books already mentioned in Chapter Two continued to be used, and to wax or wane in importance as the months passed. *B is for Bear* and *A Story to Tell* (both by Dick Bruna), continued to play an important role in Cushla's reading life, and both *The Owl and the Pussycat* and *The House that Jack Built* never failed to entertain her.

Bill Martin's *Brown Bear, Brown Bear* was introduced at about eleven months, and achieved immediate success. This book uses a repetitive device to tie together, in rhymed couplets, a list of likely and unlikely animals – a black sheep, a blue horse, a purple cat:

> Brown bear, brown bear, what do you see?
> I see a yellow duck looking at me.
> Yellow duck, yellow duck, what do you see? . . .

It seems likely that from Cushla's point of view *Brown Bear* had everything. It embodied the clear, bright no-background illustrations of the Bruna books, and the repetitive jaunty rhyme of *The House that Jack Built*. At all events, it slid easily into favour at this time.

Cushla could now sit firmly on an adult knee and, along with her growing dexterity at pointing and page-turning, could smack a page enthusiastically to show approval. Presumably, she could also have pushed a book away if she did not want a story. This never happened; looking at books continued to take pride of place among her occupations.

When Cushla was eleven months old, her mother one day turned *B is for Bear* upside down while she was intently examining a page. Immediately Cushla tried to turn her head full-circle in order to restore the normal order. Later this reaction was tested by presenting other upside down pictures from familiar books, without first showing the correct orientation. Without fail, the baby recognised the incongruity and tried to compensate by arranging her head appropriately. (By fifteen months this had become a game, and Cushla could say 'upside down' (pronouncing it 'uppa-tida-darna'). This accomplishment was usually greeted with astonished amusement by visitors, and became almost a party trick, Cushla laughing too, and enjoying the attention.)

Quite suddenly, at about a year old, she began to sound the initial letter of separate nouns as she pointed to pictures. Again, it was *B is for Bear* that provided the stimulus. Cushla, with eyes close to the book and finger pointing, would breathe 'fff' when the fish appeared, 'p' for the pig, etc. This seemed at the time unusual, and there seems no precedent for it in the literature. Indeed there is some evidence for the reverse.

Zhurova (1963) performed a series of experiments on teaching pre-school children (three to seven) to analyse words in terms of single sounds. The results showed that, initially, the youngest children could not understand what was meant by 'the first sound'. In trying to isolate it, they produced a sort of stutter, almost invariably then producing the whole word, as in 'd-d-doggie'. Again, Brown and Bellugi (1964), noting that very young children required to imitate a model's utterances constantly retain 'contentives' (those parts of speech which carry semantic content or meaning) in preference to other words, suggest that this in part arises from the fact that stress is placed on these words in pronunciation. Thus, from a sentence, 'this is a fish', the child would retain 'fish' and the stressed part of 'fish' is surely the soft 'i', in combination with either the 'f' before, or the final 'sh'. At seventeen months, when tested, Cushla clearly produced the unvoiced sounds s, p and f, and the nasal 'm' for, respectively, pictures of a sailor, a pig, a fish and a mouse. One can say with some certainty that this retention was unusual.

Four books in the Burke Home-Start series were introduced at this time because they possessed features already described – bright simple pictures against a clear (in this case, white) background, with simple text. These, all by Eileen Ryder and illustrated by L. A. Ivory, were: *Whose Baby Is It?*, *Who Are We?*, *What Do We Like?* and *What Colour Is It?*

Each of these small (16 cm × 16 cm) books is similarly designed. One-sentence statements describe a simple picture, in each case answering the question posed by the title: "Butter is yellow, and so are lemons" (from *What Colour Is It?*). Clarity is the keynote; the people, animals and objects have a Lenski-like immobility, a starkness of outline against the white page which, presumably, aided Cushla's perception. After intently examining the picture at close quarters, she would bring her eyes across or down to the print, focusing carefully on it with obvious interest.

Her cousin, Samuel, four months older, demonstrated quite different reactions to these and similar books. Like Cushla exposed to books from babyhood, but by contrast a vigorous, active child who could at fifteen months walk, climb, and manipulate objects with some dexterity, he would give each page a cursory inspection, perhaps point to an object which took his eye, name it in his incoherent language, and turn the page as soon as possible. Indeed, page-turning rather than picture-inspection often seemed to be Samuel's preference.

Observation of other children of this age leads to the conclusion that this, rather than Cushla's reaction, is the normal one. One can only theorise that Cushla's book behaviour had developed in response to her own individual needs, and the way in which they had been met by the adults in her life. It is not possible to suggest reasons for her intense interest in print itself except to speculate that, given her poor eye co-ordination, sharply etched shapes against a light background constituted a clearly visible image. Certainly, and for whatever reason, Cushla does seem to have been, by comparison with the average child, unusually interested in symbols from an early age.

Two books by Lois Lenski were added to Cushla's library at this time: *Davy's Day* and *Papa Small*. Both of these titles have been in print continuously for thirty years; both must be regarded as classics. Lenski's square little characters may seem unimaginative to adults and their activities mundane, but they enable the young child to see, perhaps for the first time, that life goes on between the covers of a book.

"Davy wakes up early. He brushes his teeth and washes his face. He eats his breakfast." Each page, right to the end of the book, when he "takes a bath, reads a good book or two . . .", faithfully mirrors the

35

two-year-old's activities through the day. *Papa Small* describes the weekly round of a family – Papa Small, Mama Small, Polly Small, Paul Small and Baby Small – who work, play, go shopping, and go to church on Sunday, where "Baby Small cries and has to be taken out".

Again, the illustrations have clear outlines against a white background with simple text on an otherwise blank page, facing the picture. It is unlikely that Cushla, at fifteen months, understood much of the text of either book. Her experience was even more limited than that of a healthy normal child of like age. But she loved listening, and she examined the pictures minutely. And Davy's "good book or two" must surely have struck a chord!

The Noisy Book represents something of a departure in young children's books. Each page illustrates a noise – a soldier with a drum, a boy with a violin, a barber cutting hair, or simply an animal. In each case the appropriate sound meanders across the page in large black letters: *Ratatata . . . eeeweeoo-oo-ee! Oink-oink!* Cushla found this book funny – mainly, it must be admitted, because it presented an opportunity for the officiating adult to use his or her histrionic talent in noise-making. In fact, it can be handled only by an adult who is prepared to perform! As such it is a splendid vehicle for the furtherance of a relationship, and Cushla loved the experience.

Two of the Bowmar Manipulative Books were introduced at this time, in an effort to encourage her to use her hands. *Where Is Home?* is a 'flap' book, each page opening out to reveal the rest of the picture and answer a question: "Where is home for the cat? Where is home for the baby chicks?" Cushla quickly learned the trick, and showed great delight and satisfaction in unearthing the hidden portion of each picture.

Little, Big, Bigger has pages of varying width. Successive turning of pages reveals "a little elephant, a big elephant, a bigger elephant" by the ingenious trick of detaching half the original object by turning the first, narrow page, to reveal a much larger portion underneath. This gimmick, clever in itself and infinitely attractive to the slightly older child, was not quite as successful as the less sophisticated trick in *Where Is Home?*, but, with its clear bright pictures and stout stiff pages, the book encouraged Cushla to turn the leaves, and achieved considerable success. It was to become a great favourite several months later, at about two.

But Where Is the Green Parrot? by Thomas and Wanda Zacharias was introduced just before eighteen months to give Cushla practice at finding an object which was not clearly apparent. The green parrot is progressively well hidden as this book proceeds; first he perches conspicuously on the red roof of the house which has ". . . a blue door with a latch, a yellow balcony with flowerpots . . .", but later he is concealed in a vase of flowers which camouflage him superbly, and then in a bushy tree. Cushla had to have help the first time; thereafter she scanned each picture carefully, finding the parrot with great satisfaction.

Cushla's way of showing enthusiasm at this time included a habit of flapping both hands in the air and laughing delightedly. This involved removing her eyes from the book; she would then drop her hands and once again bring her eyes close to the page in order to focus. The effort required to do this would change her mood from gaiety to seriousness; extracting the meaning from books was a sober business.

At seventeen months, Cushla was tested at the clinic of the Education Department, University of Auckland. Both the Gesell Development Schedule and the Denver Developmental Screening Test were administered.

For purposes of comparison, we quote here the results of the Gesell test, which had also been given at thirty-five weeks.

On the personal-social test, Cushla now performed at a fourteen-months-old level, as against her actual age of seventeen months. Her 'adaptive' score (skill at 'fine hand motor tasks, guided by eyes') was assessed at six months, her gross (large muscle) motor skills at nine months and her language at twelve months.

The following comments were appended by the psychologist:

The pattern was one of slight retardation in the personal-social and language areas. The clear developmental lag in gross motor scores and particularly in fine motor-adaptive scores was associated with abnormal reactions of the hands and arms and with unusual visual behaviour.

Three different levels of functioning in hand-arm behaviour were noted.

1) Involuntary movements occurred – hands flew up in the air, objects were held momentarily and then flung out and back as the hand (usually the right) released them.

2) Appropriate voluntary movements were carried out with concentration and effort – blowing a whistle, shaking a rattle, orienting to a picture book.

3) Book behaviour, trained by adults in her family, was very advanced. She peered at the book at close quarters, scanned the pictures with her eyes, uttered appropriate sounds for some pictures without prompting (s, sailor; m, mouse; p, pig; f, fish) and turned the pages – a fine motor co-ordination task.

(I checked this carefully because it was inconsistent with the rest of the record.)

Cushla's personal-social score had improved somewhat in the eight and a half months that had elapsed since her first test at thirty-five weeks (see Chapter Two). On the Gesell scale, she now achieved a level three months below her chronological age. It seems likely that her difficulties of focus and orientation were still inhibiting her in this area, as in others. However, the higher scores (as against her earlier achievement of a twenty-four-week personal-social level at thirty-five weeks) probably mirrored a greater involvement with people and things than had been possible earlier.

Cushla's sleeping pattern was still erratic in the extreme. At no time during the night did she sleep peacefully, and never for longer than several hours at a time. It seemed impossible to keep her covered, due to her disturbed tossing, and she would wake constantly in a distressed condition.

No systematic programme of coping with this situation was ever evolved, although different ways were tried. The use of drugs was abandoned, as mentioned earlier, because of its effect on her subsequent alertness, and no one way of inducing her to return to sleep seemed always to succeed. Sometimes a bottle of warm milk would help, whereas at other times it was necessary to take her from bed and amuse her until she fell asleep, usually while listening to a story. It is likely that this factor, leading to almost constant over-tiredness, affected Cushla's development in the area of personal-social performance.

The Denver Developmental Screening Test, given at the same time, revealed substantially the same picture, the only marked difference being that, on this test, Cushla's language score was exactly normal: that is, she had achieved at seventeen months the level expected of a normal child of that age.

This discrepancy on the language tests was probably due to chance inattention or lack of co-operation during the administration of the first test, or may actually have revealed some retardation. No conclusion is possible – but it is easy to imagine that Cushla, with her difficulties of focus and orientation, may have failed to demonstrate her full capacity on any given test.

Her 'clear developmental lag in gross motor scores, and particularly in fine motor adaptive scores' was plainly revealed; Cushla achieved a six-months score on each test, as against seventeen months' actual age. The normal child of seventeen months walks well, and is often beginning to run unsteadily. He is able to push and pull toys, and can sit on a step, or a small chair, by a process of backing into it. None of these accomplishments was available to Cushla – but surprisingly, she could turn the pages of a book, one by one: 'a fine motor co-ordination task', as the report itself states. (It should be noted that, for page-turning, Cushla used a wrist-flicking motion which was uncharacteristic of the average seventeen-month-old child's gross arm-hand use. This was necessitated by the weakness of her arm, which always lay on a flat surface during this process.)

The appended comment beginning 'Book behaviour, trained by adults in her family, was very advanced . . .' (see above) is to be seen for what it was – the honest and slightly astonished recognition on the part of the psychologist that specific training in a narrow field had overcome motor limitations which might ordinarily be regarded as prohibitive to such accomplishment.

39

Cushla and her books

In the field of book behaviour, Cushla was clearly surmounting the handicaps of 'abnormal reactions of hands and arms' and 'unusual visual behaviour' which had beset her since birth, and which were noted in these tests.

The fact that Cushla performed specific tasks – blowing a whistle, shaking a rattle – 'with concentration and effort' was consistent with her everyday behaviour. Concentration on a set task was characteristic; she was accustomed to being shown how to do something and helped to succeed.

The period from nine to eighteen months saw Cushla progress from a position which gave little hope for subsequent development to a point from which improvement might be expected.

The baby's success in rolling over and her subsequent attempts (however unsuccessful) to crawl, introduced a note of hope which would have seemed unjustified earlier, but which now lent support to the family's growing conviction that she was a child of considerable determination. Spontaneous practice in physical skills was constantly interrupted by spells of illness requiring antibiotic treatment, and she must also have been overtired almost continuously. Nonetheless, she kept trying, with steady, if unspectacular, results.

The evidence that she was able to recognise that a picture was inverted at eleven months is incontrovertible. It seems, therefore, that such recognition is possible at this age, although unusual. Certainly, Sanchia, Cushla's younger sister, gave no sign of recognising that a picture in a familiar book was upside down when tested at eleven months.

Watson (1964) devised and carried out three experiments to determine whether infants under six months would evidence object orientation perception by smiling differentially at different orientations of the human face, and, as an extension of this, 'to assess object-orientation perception by a means other than the relatively object-specific response of smiling'. Among several other findings, Watson concludes that 'the capacity to perceive orientation appears well-established by the fourteenth week'. However, he makes a distinction between the results obtained when using a human face or a pictured human face, and other symbols, stating that 'any significance of orientation for the (other forms) . . . was unobserved, while the same contrast in orientation of the facial stimuli had marked effects'.

Of significance is Watson's concluding question as to 'whether the infants saw the difference in orientation but did not care, or whether they were simply unable to see the contrast in orientation with these particular non-facial forms'. The answer to this, he admits, he does not know.

It is likely, then, that Sanchia saw the difference in orientation but simply 'did not care', whereas Cushla, with more limited activities available to her and therefore more heavily reliant on pictured images for her information, did care, and, when denied correct orientation, attempted to compensate by turning her head.

During this time, up to eighteen months, Cushla was still occupied with page-by-page books, although the two Lenski titles, *Davy's Day* and *Papa Small*, might have been expected to engender the idea that a character on successive pages is the same character – an idea which must clearly be grasped if the story proper is to have meaning at the next stage. There is some evidence that Cushla had grasped this idea; Davy was quickly identified on each page, Cushla using her new-found skill with intense concentration, to point him out. The stage was certainly set for the introduction of real stories, with theme, plot, and climax.

This period closes with Cushla at eighteen months, her handicaps still unexplained and not all identified. But whereas at nine months her parents had been almost afraid to contemplate the future, fearing that for Cushla it might not exist, now they found themselves making plans for her and speculating daily on her growing needs.

For, against all odds, Cushla was becoming a happy child. Constantly beset with illness, subjected to painful medical procedures and periods when even her parents' arms offered small protection from an incomprehensibly bleak world, she was nonetheless emerging as a child of spirit and spontaneity, prepared to laugh and enjoy the good times, and bounce back from the bad.

Chapter Four

EIGHTEEN MONTHS TO THREE YEARS

The first twelve months of this period saw no improvement in Cushla's health, and two short periods in hospital were necessary. However, the identification of her genetic defect early in the period, while it provided no real guide to future treatment, at least ended speculation; given the fact that every cell in Cushla's body contained an abnormality, and that this abnormality had led to her physical and mental defects, then the only possible course was one of constant individual care and instruction. The family conviction that Cushla should develop her unknown potential to the furthest possible extent was, if anything, intensified.

A series of chromosome tests was administered to Cushla in June 1973. The results showed a faint divergence from normal which was dismissed as probably due to imperfect samples; the chance of such an abnormality appearing in a child of normal parents was extremely remote. This information was conveyed to Cushla's parents and reassurance expressed. However, the parents were not satisfied. Both had had scientific training and required definite information as to the possibility of their having another defective child. At their urging, the hospital agreed to repeat the test, and this time to test both parents as well.

The results were clear; Cushla and her father both showed faulty chromosome patterns, a fact that was reaffirmed at once by re-testing. Tests were then administered to Stephen's parents with negative results. The only possible conclusion was that, at Stephen's conception, a mutation had occurred which led to the rearrangement of the chromosomes within each cell.

Every normal human cell contains forty-six chromosomes, each of which is made up of a chain of genes. These genes carry the hereditary factors.

Twenty-three of the chromosomes in every cell have, through a process of division and reduction at conception, come from the mother, and twenty-three from the father.

In Stephen's case, two chromosomes of the forty-six show abnormality; one is longer, and one shorter, than the other forty-four. However, the full complement of genes is present in each cell, the total number of genes carried by the one long and one short chromosome being equal to that usually divided equally between two normal-length chromosomes. Thus Cushla's father shows no abnormality and is, indeed, an exceptionally healthy and intelligent young man. Complications, however, might be expected to arise when, at the conception of his child, Stephen's abnormally arranged chromosomes joined in random combination with those of his wife.

Diagrams showing both Cushla's parents' chromosome patterns, and the possible patterns for their children, are given in Appendix C.

In effect, Cushla's parents had one chance in four of producing a completely normal child, unable to transmit the defect.

Again, their chances of producing an apparently normal child (identical genetically to its father, but able to transmit the defect) were one in four.

It is worth noting here that, in either of these eventualities, there would have been no way of detecting the abnormality, and the parents would certainly have had another child – with the same chance of normality, and danger of the undetected defect being passed to the next generation.

A child of Cushla's genetic make-up again constituted a one-in-four chance, and the fourth combination, resulting in a foetus with inadequate chromosome make-up for the production of a live child, was also a one-in-four chance.

It can be seen, therefore, that abnormality, concealed or apparent, was a two-in-three chance, given a viable foetus.

By twenty-one months, Cushla could take a few unsteady steps between two sets of adult arms. She had acquired little balance, but demonstrated her usual willingness to 'give it a go', making small complaint at occasional bumps. Convulsions caused by a severe flu infection led to her returning to hospital for three days at this time, and resulted in a slowing up of the walking process, but by twenty-four months she could walk unsteadily for short distances. By thirty months she was walking constantly, although in a very unco-ordinated fashion. Her characteristic stance was one of slight backward-leaning, with arms bent, swinging out and back at shoulder level, and head pushed forward to improve balance.

The uselessness of her arms during falls, and her general unsteadiness, led to constant accidents. It became difficult at this time to strike a balance between the sort of supervision which would have inhibited her practice, and total freedom, with consequent accident.

The average child walks without support at approximately fourteen months, and at twenty-four months, a stage at which Cushla was walking unsteadily for short distances, walks firmly with total body co-ordination, running quite well and seldom falling. Nonetheless, there was reason for satisfaction in Cushla's performance; earlier medical prognoses had been consistently pessimistic, on both physical and intellectual counts, and Cushla's consistent passing of milestones provided more hope for the future than her family had dared harbour, before this time. Cushla's crawling did not improve; her arms were still too weak to support her body and she obviously found the process uncomfortable and unsatisfactory (see note in brackets, page 32).

This quite possibly lent her walking attempts some impetus; she clearly intended to become mobile. Hand and arm mastery continued to make slow progress during this period. By eighteen months Cushla could take a light wooden or plastic block from a box, but would almost always drop it before her hand reached its destination. At twenty-three months she learned, after concentrated instruction, to drop small blocks into a wide shallow plastic container. Before this, although her grasp had become stronger, her hand did not seem to react to the 'release' order from her brain.

From the age of two-and-a-half, Cushla's mother took her, each week, to a small heated swimming pool where lessons were being given to older pre-schoolers. Although Cushla was too young to be enrolled, permission was given for her to join the group, provided her mother swam with her. It was quickly apparent that she was able and willing to follow instructions and had no fear of the water, or of putting her head beneath the surface. Swimming, from early days had been seen as a potentially valuable therapy for Cushla. It was felt that a good start had been made.

No thought had been given so far to toilet training. Cushla's poor muscular condition, her frequent periods of illness, the time-consuming nature of her care, and, in particular, her liability to bladder infection and her known kidney defect banished all possibility of such training earlier. However, by thirty-three months it was apparent that she was often dry for such long periods that training might be appropriate. In fact, Cushla learned both bladder and bowel control within a week, though she has continued to need napkins at night.

By contrast, the average child has control of both bladder and bowel at two, although many children who might conform to this standard fail to, for various reasons. They may resist parental urging in order to assert their own personalities, play with such concentration that they frequently forget, or simply take longer to develop the necessary physiological mechanisms of control. Cushla's achievement of bladder and bowel control at thirty-three months is therefore to be seen as near-normal – particularly as there was room for conjecture that, with earlier parental intervention, earlier achievement might have resulted.

At two years of age, Cushla was able to join the Devonport Play Centre. Other families from the playgroup formed a year before also transferred at about this time, thus ensuring continuity of friendships already established. Although still able to participate only in a limited way, Cushla enjoyed the experience and both she and her parents profited from the involvement in a congenial group.

The number of books with which Cushla was familiar grew rapidly after eighteen months. Two more Bruna books, *Snuffy* and *The*

King, proved just as popular as the earlier examples and *Davy and His Dog* (Lenski), featuring the same Davy as "read a good book or two", somewhat older and equipped with an engaging dog, became a great favourite.

Another Lenski title *The Little Farm* again demonstrated this author's perennial, and (to adults) somewhat mystifying appeal to the very young.

Helping at Home and *Puppies and Kittens*, two Ladybird Books, were introduced at this time, as they seemed to fill Cushla's growing need for identification of familiar objects and activities in her books. The former shows two children doing dishes, hanging out washing, sweeping the floor, – activities which Cushla could not undertake with any skill, but with which she was involved nonetheless.

I have found it interesting – in fact, fascinating – to compare Cushla's interaction with books and storytelling, from the age of two onwards, with that of Carol, Dorothy Neal White's daughter of the same age as reported in *Books Before Five* (New Zealand Council for Educational Research, 1954).

Carol and Cushla were born, each late in the year, twenty-six years apart. Carol was born into the cultured home of parents already deeply involved with books; her mother's earlier book, *About Books for Children* (1946), reflected some years' experience as children's librarian at the Dunedin Public Library, a position to which she was appointed in 1937. She had been chosen the previous year as one of two New Zealanders to be trained at the Carnegie Library School in Pittsburgh. Carol herself was a healthy, highly intelligent child. At two years of age, when the diary account began, she was already articulate and involved. Her experience of books clearly complemented her daily life; an entry made when she was two years four months mentioned her increased enjoyment of farm animals in her books after her first experience of the real thing, but noted her growing willingness to take on trust pictures of unfamiliar objects: "Whereas at eighteen months she had not been interested in *any* pictures of things she hadn't seen, now at two she is willing to look at a picture of something she hasn't met in real life."

46

Cushla, with her near-total inability to enjoy the normal activities of Carol and her friend Ann, was much less discriminating; her alternatives were far fewer than Carol's, her recourse to books accordingly more constant, and her attitude less selective. Then again, Cushla's expectations of understanding, her demand for meaning, would not, at that stage, have approached Carol's in depth or extent. Cushla still contended with unknowable handicaps, sensory and physical; she was still, in essence, cut off. The swift, almost undetectable exchange between the normal child and her environment, the sense in which all experience is 'grist to her mill', simply did not apply to Cushla.

Dorothy White also mentions, at this period, Carol's increasing preference for coloured illustrations over black and white – Carol ". . . wanted to waste no time with penny plain, but to leap on to tuppence coloured" – although she notes that Lois Lenski's *Let's Play House* (now unobtainable), which at first she thought "mediocre, with its quite ordinary black and white pictures", had been requested and read ten or twelve times during the preceding week. Cushla, of course, had always responded with close attention to black and white illustrations and, in particular, to black letters or numbers on a white background. It is likely, however, that clearness of outline mattered for Cushla more than for Carol and that this constituted the significant constant factor in Cushla's favourite books. Certainly, this factor is present in the Lenski and Bruna books, in Peppé's *House that Jack Built*, the two Ladybird Books, the Home-Start books and the Bowmar Manipulative titles.

Cushla's speech at this time was still largely confined to the use of nouns and verbs, but it was clear by two-and-a-half years that her understood vocabulary was fairly extensive. Books with simple, well-rounded stories now achieved prominence. *Harry the Dirty Dog* by Gene Zion and *Mr Gumpy's Outing* by John Burningham were both followed attentively, again and again, and *The Box with Red Wheels* made an auspicious comeback. Beatrix Potter appeared for the second time in Cushla's reading life with *The Story of a Fierce Bad Rabbit* and Minarik's enchanting *Little Bear* stories, illustrated by Maurice Sendak, were listened to with rapt attention. These books have certain features in common which go far to ensure enduring success with the very young.

To begin with, they have appropriateness of theme, or subject matter. Children between the ages of eighteen months and three years are becoming increasingly conscious of the world about them, and appreciate accurate representation of that world. But this must take place through the agency of known objects and backgrounds if identification is to be complete. For Cushla, as for most of her peers, a pet dog who got so dirty that he changed from "a white dog with black spots to a black dog with white spots" is totally comprehensible – and the phrase itself, its one-syllable nouns and adjectives adroitly interchanged, may perhaps be their first experience of that special pleasure which the sharply honed expression has for the human ear.

For this is the second requirement of books for the very young: a use of words that have precision and yet explore the resources of language, deftly and eloquently setting the scene and moving the action along. Not many writers can do this; not many editors recognise its essentiality for the very young.

And the story itself should proceed in a straight line. Tangents and diversions are not for the one-to-three-year-old. He is merely confused by extra information, and loses the thread.

Mr Gumpy serves as the classic example: beautifully paced, each character coming alive through his action and speech, with no need for description:

> "May I come please, Mr Gumpy?" said the pig.
> "Very well, but don't muck about . . ."

Of course, he does muck about, as we all know he will, and contributes with the children (who squabble), the chickens (who flap) and the goat (who kicks), to the predictable capsize of the boat. But there is no comment, no moralising, no need for pardon; all is implicit in the action, the dialogue, and of course, the illustrations.

The satisfying nature of climax, for the two-year-old as for the adult, hardly needs explanation – or perhaps, defies it. Description must be resorted to. Climax surely consists of a sensation of resolution, a summit reached inevitably, deliciously anticipated, all-sufficing on arrival. Again, it is an experience which fits a child out for his future with books; he is armed, he has added to his repertoire of response. One might almost suggest that his critical faculty has been prodded into life, for this early contact with the best surely presupposes later stirrings of impatience at the trite and the shoddy.

Cushla's continuing affection for rhyme, as seen since early days in *The Owl and the Pussycat*, *The House that Jack Built* and more recently *Hush Little Baby*, led her parents to try A. A. Milne at about two-and-a-half years. From first contact, Cushla listened with absorption, even when the text was beyond her understanding, focusing intently on the page and peering at Ernest Shepard's small black and white line drawings. (This was to be the beginning of a long attachment. To the time of writing, *When We Were Very Young* has never been superseded in her affections.)

Play With Me, a quietly illustrated, deceptively simple story, was first introduced at this time and has survived the reigns of other more flamboyant books to become an enduring favourite. In it a little girl, who looks strangely like Cushla herself, invites successive small animals to play with her. All seem unenthusiastic, but one after the other they come back to join her, just as despair sets in.

Each full-page picture shows the same scene with minor but significant changes in grouping. The 'action' is almost discernible from the pictures alone, so carefully and perceptively is each change in gesture or movement portrayed.

Marie Hall Ets, in all her books, demonstrates a sensitive awareness of the concerns of young childhood which is regrettably absent from the work of many modern authors. She encapsulates the small child's limited vision and sees the world from child height: the grasshopper on the leaf, the frog on the ground. She knows, and believes in, the importance of making friends.

Play With Me was published in 1955 and has been constantly in print in an American edition ever since. Since 1977 it has been published as a Puffin.

Cushla and her books

My Brother Sean by Petronella Breinburg could not offer a greater contrast, with its startling, vivid pictures of a small black boy and his experience in beginning play school. But it speaks directly to the very young, giving tongue to universal hopes and fears (though Carol, who was puzzled by Rose Fyleman's 'I think mice are nice', asking 'Who thinks?', might equally have asked 'Whose brother Sean?' if it had been written in time for her three-year-old perusal).

Between two-and-a-half and three years, Cushla (less linguistically critical) requested constant rereadings. She had several times been left for short periods (always with a close friend of her parents who knew her well) at Play Centre, and perhaps understood Sean's ambivalence to the idea – despair at his mother's departure mixed with the attraction of exciting play equipment. Cushla solicitously kissed his howling little face at every reading, and beamed with relief when he finally "smiled a teeny-weeny smile". The phrase "teeny-weeny smile" repeated over and over became a chant at the time, and she was always anxious to reach this part of the story. Her identification with Sean was complete.

The Tale of Peter Rabbit was an instant success at two years nine months. Remembering that Dorothy White had described Carol's reaction to this book in detail, I consulted *Books Before Five* and was interested to find that this was exactly the stage at which, newly introduced, it had become "in our family, as in thousands of others, a classic bedtime story". How many more thousands have been added in the intervening quarter-century between Carol and Cushla's capitulation to its perennial charm!

Unlike Carol, Cushla has never been worried by the absence of part of a character or object in a picture – in this case, Peter's body, hidden in the watering can; only his ears protrude. 'Where is the rest of him?' asked Carol. Cushla did not enquire, so her mother asked her. 'In there,' said Cushla firmly, pointing to the can. Could her intense concentration on the pictured image from such an early age have given her at least one advantage over the child whose energies were properly devoted to many pursuits from which she was excluded?

Eric Carle's *The Very Hungry Caterpillar* has probably made more impact on the New Zealand public than any other picture book in the

50

last ten years; it has certainly had record sales. Cushla encountered it just before she turned three, and echoed the reaction of thousands of other three-year-olds when she immediately demanded, 'Read it again'. It is easy to see what this book has; it is harder to understand the exact nature of its superlative appeal. It certainly has form, unity, colour and climax, and it lists delectable foods that children enjoy. Adults approve of its built-in nature lesson (the stages from caterpillar to "beautiful butterfly" are faithfully documented) and its unobtrusive counting slant —"On Monday he ate *one* apple but he was still hungry. On Tuesday he ate *two* pears" —and the opportunity it presents for painless learning of the days of the week.

But children are seldom, if ever, seduced into accepting their parents' judgement on these issues. It has repetition, and we believe that this is beneficial (we know it is popular), and each stiff, robust page has a bonus in the shape of a finger-sized hole to show where the caterpillar went. The whole is beautifully bound and produced: a work of art. Cushla saw it in perspective; she liked it, but was not bowled over. And most of her reading time, suddenly, must be devoted to *Grandmother Lucy and Her Hats*, at any rate, leaving time only for *Harry, Mr Gumpy, Peter Rabbit* and endless sorties into the poetry of A. A. Milne.

Cushla first met *Grandmother Lucy and Her Hats* when she was nearly three. Speculation since as to why this book was chosen does not reveal the answer; it was longer than any story she had listened to before and, as well as introducing several unfamiliar objects and ideas (an attic, squeaking hinges, cobwebs), used language which in parts was quite complex. Of Tom, the cat, and the geraniums, she heard: "He nudged them with his nose, and tiptoed round them with his careful feet, and smiled at them with his shining eyes." And of the contents of a trunk: "Sometimes a violin, or silk that didn't want to leave my fingers, or a little pointed boot with a row of buttons, or a brown photograph."

Frank Francis's illustrations are delectable in the extreme; each open spread is planned as a whole, the text placed with artistry in the white spaces. The colours are clear and bright, without harshness, and the people and objects stand out sharply; there is no difficulty in separating one from the other. They have something of Beatrix Potter's precision and clarity, the whole bigger and brighter but with the same attention to detail.

The story flows, the introduction setting the pattern: "Grand-mother Lucy was a very, very old Grandmother, and she lived in a house with red roses. . . . When I went to see her, I knocked at her door. The door was thick and squeaked, and she always said, 'We must oil the hinges.' We never did, so it squeaked and she smiled and I went in." Perhaps this story served two purposes for Cushla, its homely detail confirming her own experience – with grandmother, cat, and tea with "your favourite cakes" – and the touch of glamour, in Grandmother Lucy's succession of hats, extending and expanding that experience. At all events, it had immediate and lasting effect; before long Cushla had it by heart, and phrase after phrase appeared in her con-versation: "books in toppling towers", applied to her own books, "slippery buttons", "dandelion clock".

Six months later, on being asked after her operation to show her own grandmother how she could remove the dressing on the wound before her bath, she tried, found that it was sticking tightly, and said, "I can't – not even to please Grandmother", a phrase straight from *Grandmother Lucy*.

Referring again to Dorothy White's diary, I wondered at Cushla's endless acceptance of what must often have been incomprehensible. Carol at this age required "an immense amount of explaining", whereas Cushla seemed to accept the words as they came.

Although she listened intently, she seemed often to be letting the words wash over her, rather than sink in. Carol's greater insistence on immediate clarification of the unfamiliar plainly indicated a penetrating intelligence, her development outstripping Cushla's at the same age. But perhaps they were intrinsically children of very different bent – Carol with the need to *know* before she moved on, Cushla with her apparent willingness to listen almost endlessly often, surely, without understanding? Dorothy White says about her daughter, at three, speaking of her rejection of Lear's *Nonsense Songs* . . . "her distaste may come from the fact that she has heard very little spoken to her that has been quite incomprehensible. It is as though she expects words to mean something in an obvious and substantial way. . . ."

Remembering Cushla's continuing affection for Lear's *Owl and the Pussycat* and her immediate capitulation to A. A. Milne's rhythmic verse, one is inclined to feel that her enjoyment may have been almost entirely sensory. And this enjoyment, surely, must be accepted as part and parcel of human experience, known, believed in, and yet inexplicable. The love of words, of language sensitively used and spoken, has its counterpart in the love of music, appealing to the senses, unnecessary of elucidation. It is no more accessible to all human beings than is the intense feeling that is evoked for some by music; but it exists, with a validity that defies analysis. It is certainly true that children display as wide a range of language sensitivity as of musical response.

But one is driven to wonder at the difference in ready availability of meaning for Carol and Cushla, the one superbly equipped, the other battling (unself-consciously so far) with formidable handicaps. It is difficult, in the circumstances, to discount the possibility that the need to compensate was an ingredient of Cushla's willingness to listen, often without understanding; or that 'listening' also meant the opportunity to 'look', an opportunity not always available to the child of limited vision, and not to be missed.

Cushla was exactly two years eight months on the day that the family triumphantly bore home her small adopted sister Sanchia, eight days old. 'Baby Sister' quickly became an accepted part of the household; mercifully, from the first day, she ate, slept, ate and slept again, passing all of *her* milestones in record time, and quickly becoming an assertive little personality in her own right. Her addition to the family has brought about a lessening of tension; it is not possible for Cushla's parents to worry all the time about her any longer. They have a second child with a claim to their love and attention, and any lingering suspicion that they were incapable of raising a cheerful, healthy child has long since disappeared.

In September, 1974, when two years nine months old, Cushla was tested by the Psychological Service of the Department of Education at Auckland University. The Denver Developmental Screening Test was administered.

Cushla's personal-social score was estimated at between six and eight months below her actual age – that is, at between twenty-five and twenty-seven months, as against thirty-three months. In this area, the report mentions 'some unevenness' noting that Cushla was 'able to help in some household tasks, but was not able to dress without supervision'.

In this particular test, fine and gross motor skills were assessed together, Cushla performing at a twenty-two-months-old level as against her actual age of thirty-three months.

In language development, the test revealed that she had achieved a normal level for a child of two years and nine months, her actual age.

Cushla's most marked improvement since her last tests at seventeen months was in the fine motor-adaptive area.

At seventeen months her performance at the six-months level constituted extreme retardation, whereas now, performing at the twenty-two-months level when actually aged thirty-three months, she had clearly made up ground.

Although still very unco-ordinated, Cushla was running and climbing, and riding a small tricycle of the type which is propelled by the action of the feet on the ground.

Surprisingly, she could turn a somersault, although she had not sufficient spring to be able to land in a sitting position. This accomplishment, at this time, attracted some admiration from other children at Play Centre, many of whom, although better endowed physically than Cushla, had not the confidence to attempt a somersault.

She was now able to place small pegs in holes in a pegboard, and scribble enthusiastically with large crayons on plain newsprint. Simple wooden jigsaw puzzles still defied her efforts, but it was clear that she knew that the pieces were meant to go together and, often, that she could recognise the relationship of two pieces (such as the hand and arm of person). A wooden puzzle having nine identical circles each fitting into matching holes provided Cushla with her first real success at puzzles, and gave practice in the fine motor skill of lifting the pieces by grasping the knob on top of each. This puzzle also provided colour-matching practice; each flat circle was painted in the same colour as one of the shallow holes. A child might at first position the circles without attention to colour, later stretching to this extra skill. Cushla quickly mastered this puzzle, matching the colours with some satisfaction, although still naming them indiscriminately.

In terms of language development, Cushla had made her greatest surge forward. The report noted that she used 'combinations of words, plurals etc'. Her enunciation was still not very clear, and she still used the pronoun 'me' instead of 'I' as subject of a sentence – 'Me do that, now'. She had never used her own name as some children do (as in 'Cushla do that') although she could produce her full name and address if asked.

Cushla's lack of expertise in dressing herself reflected her continuing inability to use her hands and arms with the deftness that characterises the normal child approaching three years of age. But constant, though slow, improvement was taking place, and her temperament undeniably helped; although often fractious and miserable, because unwell, she seldom displayed the angry reaction to frustration that might have been expected.

It should be remembered that Cushla still spent days at a time too ill to take an active interest in her surroundings and still slept only spasmodically, her breathing difficult and heavy. Twice in this year she was admitted to hospital. Each time, her usual ill-health had deteriorated to a frightening level requiring emergency action.

It was noted by the psychologist who tested her at two years nine months that she was 'most co-operative in the test situation'. Those who knew her well at this time would agree that this statement well described Cushla's approach to life and learning. One could count on Cushla to *try*.

This period saw Cushla's attainment of a language level appropriate to her chronological age, and considerable progress on other fronts. The discovery and identification of her genetic defect, as mentioned earlier, while it established that some of her handicaps (notably her

55

co-ordinatory difficulties) were irreversible, at least ended speculation; and there was reason to hope that future training would ameliorate, if not remove, some of her difficulties.

The step forward into the world of 'real stories' had been taken triumphantly. Beginning with Bruna's *Snuffy* and *The King* and proceeding by way of Lenski's *Davy and His Dog* and *The Little Farm* to *Harry the Dirty Dog, Mr Gumpy's Outing, Play With Me* and *The Tale of Peter Rabbit*, Cushla demonstrated her ability to follow a story line, understanding the action, and identifying with the characters. 'Nellie all dirty just like Harry,' she said of her grandparents' dog, at two years ten months – and her emotional reactions to the vicissitudes of Peter Rabbit's life, the boating catastrophe in *Mr Gumpy's Outing* and her anxious questions ('Where his mummy gone?' when My Brother Sean is left at playschool) left no room for doubt that she understood what was going on.

Many of Dorothy White's reports on Carol's reactions to her books confirm the normality of Cushla's responses; Carol's preference for a 'comprehensible universe' (the three kittens in *The Tale of Tom Kitten* are washed, combed, and given clean clothes when visitors are expected, a procedure with which she was familiar) echoing Cushla's satisfaction at the proposition of "visiting Grandmother" (*Grandmother Lucy and Her Hats*), a frequent occurrence in her own life.

"Everything these days must have a house and a mummy," Dorothy White reports of her daughter – and Cushla's constant question 'Where's the pussy's (dog's, baby's) mummy?' springs to mind. Both children seemed on the one hand to be enjoying their awareness of increased independence (slight, but all the more precious in Cushla's case) and on the other, needing reaffirmation of established security in which 'mummies' are just out of sight, ready to lend support.

Both children seemed fascinated by the phenomenon of night. In Carol's case *A Child's Goodnight Book* by Margaret Wise Brown provoked and reflected constant interest in 'the dark', and in Cushla's *The Animals' Lullaby* by Trude Alberti had a similar effect. The gentle, repetitive text of this book, interpreted simply but explicitly

56

by Nakatani's soft, pastel drawings, is ideal for bedtime reading. It took its place, for Cushla, beside Aliki's superb *Hush Little Baby* and *Hush-a-Bye Rhymes* edited by Anne Wood, as enduring favourites to be read as night drew in. (It was not surprising that Cushla's parents provided numerous lullaby books. There was always the chance that they might take effect!)

The differences in the children's occupations were, predictably, just as marked. Carol's activities are reported as having "increased in number, scope and duration" and again, in the early spring months of 1948, it is noted that "Carol is always busy and books have played a very small part in her life". 'Cuttings out' were said to be in fashion, and a building set much used. Neither of these dexterity-requiring occupations were as yet available to Cushla, and daily life would have been unthinkable for both mother and daughter without constant and prolonged recourse to picture books. "Where's the hospital?" asked Carol, on encountering the term for the first time. 'Hospital' had been one of Cushla's first words, its sterile precincts her second home.

There was no doubt that there had been a promising surge forward in Cushla's intellectual development in general, and language development in particular. Indeed, after two years of age, it was impossible for those closest to her to fear any longer that Cushla might be severely retarded mentally.

This certainty could not have been shared by the casual onlooker, however, for Cushla's differences from the average child were marked. Her arms were still prone to swing outwards, and her expression was often one of puzzled query. Her attempts to focus her eyes led her to move her head about frequently, and her movements were unco-ordinated. She fell often; the slightest touch seemed to knock her off balance, and she was still inclined to drop things.

In yet another way, Cushla seemed different from other children. Her experience of people had apparently, despite the pain and discomfort to which she had been subject, persuaded her that the world was a friendly place. It almost seemed that she understood that her own troubles were 'no one's fault', for she was uniformly friendly and trusting towards all people, children and adults, known and unfamiliar. It was almost as if she realised that she was unusually

57

dependent upon others and was prepared, even determined, to invoke their help.

This characteristic was, in itself, faintly worrying; the three-year-old is typically reticent until he 'knows' another person. But Cushla had experienced an unusual amount of support from a circle which had extended outwards to include not only close relatives, but friends and other Play Centre parents. What is more, in her experience, people actually enjoyed helping children. Seen against this background, her trust and friendly confidence were perhaps explicable. They were certainly fortunate, for they endeared her to a widening circle of people, enabling them to sense the questing intelligence behind the intensely focusing eyes, the determination and strength of spirit that has always been there for those who could see.

Every milestone was an achievement, in which many now seemed to share. And Cushla, despite the odds, was passing the milestones.

Chapter Five

MARCH 1975: THREE YEARS, THREE MONTHS

Cushla's health, by March 1975, was more stable than it had been at any previous stage of her life. In the previous September, she had had a severe ear and throat infection necessitating treatment with an antibiotic. Since then, her condition had improved markedly.

She was now able to run about freely, though rather disjointedly, and had achieved considerable control of her small 'hobby horse' tricycle. She still had difficulty focusing, particularly when encountering a new image, as when entering a room. On these occasions her efforts at orientation, involving energetic head movement, would sometimes deprive her of her already precarious balance. Cushla was increasingly using her hands, and it had become clear that most of her disability involved the larger arm muscles rather than the smaller hand and finger muscles. Her arms were still held, characteristically, in the outwards-and-backwards position seen since birth, and her slowness in bringing them forward to save herself, plus her very unsteady gait, led to frequent accidents. 'Watch me run fast!' had become one of her favourite injunctions; a difficult one to obey in view of her tendency to fall.

During January 1975, the family spent some time at Karekare, on the west coast near Auckland. Here, Cushla's grandparents had, several years previously, bought an acre and a half of sheltered land adjacent to the beach. On this land stood three houses – one derelict, one, built at the turn of the century, which the family was gradually repairing as a holiday home, and a third, previously used as a store and about forty years old.

The family had always loved the wildness and isolation of

Cushla and her books

Karekare, and had spent yearly holidays there since Patricia and her brothers and sisters were children.

The idea of living at Karekare permanently first occurred to Cushla's parents at this time. They were still living in a flat in Devonport, seeing little likelihood of being able to build on their own section by the sea at Paremoremo for some time to come. Now that Cushla was able to run about, the position of the flat on the first floor meant that she had to be protected from the stairs, on the one hand, and taken out to play frequently, on the other. The new baby's physical development was proceeding apace, and the time was clearly at hand when the flat would have even more severe disadvantages.

It was decided that the family should move immediately into the older house, with a view to cleaning and generally renovating the store house and making the change in due course.

This was done in late January. By the time this account begins, Patricia and Stephen, with the two little girls, had moved from the older to the newer house. Several weeks later, Patricia's sister Vivien, now teaching in Auckland, and her husband, Clive, made the decision to join them, converting the old, attached shop into a bed-sittingroom of ample proportions. Both families owned cars and there were advantages to be seen in leaving one car at Karekare for the use of the children's mother while the three working adults commuted daily to Auckland, an hour's drive away.

The household of four adults and two children settled into the small community at Karekare, and quickly made new friends. Renovations were continued, a garden started, a dog, a cat and a goat acquired. Cushla's cheeks were rosy and her small body developing a firmness it had never previously known. Sanchia, the little adopted daughter, was beautiful, intelligent and, above all, healthy. After three years of fear and uncertainty, it seemed that a calmer, more assured period was beginning.

Cushla's mother kept detailed records of her interaction with books for the month of March 1975. An attempt has been made to relate the information from these records to Cushla's increasingly complex use of language and her intellectual development generally.

One day (Monday, 3rd March) is given in full, in chart form, in the

60

Appendix. This day was chosen as typical of those days when full recording was possible.

Understandably, with a crawling seven-month-old baby as well as a demanding three-year-old, Cushla's mother was often prevented from putting pen to paper for lengthy periods during the day.

Despite difficulties however, recording was accomplished on twenty-seven days in this month.

Almost invariably, recording was immediate. Cushla's mother kept a notepad, already ruled-up, by her at all times, and concentrated on accuracy at the expense of neatness. Much of the manuscript is embellished with Cushla's 'additions'. Grubby fingermarks and a generally crumpled appearance attested its involvement in the family's daily life.

Tape recordings were made as opportunity occurred. These presented different problems, but Cushla herself grew to accept the procedure, and much useful material was collected.

By Christmas 1974, when she turned three, Cushla was showing considerable preference for 'real stories' and a number of these were introduced. *The Christmas Book* by Bruna was her first contact with the nativity story and she was enchanted. The kings and the angels in particular – square, stylised, clearly outlined little figures, their crowns and wings respectively denoting their roles – were examined, re-examined, patted, kissed and their counterparts found or imagined in a variety of likely and unlikely settings. Bruna's *The King* had, of course, been a favourite since eighteen months, and Milne's famous king who did like "a little bit of butter" with his bread was an old friend. (Cushla found his likeness in a symbolic crown-topped figure on a packet in a food-market during this month and, bent double the better to examine him, muttered, "I *do* like a little bit of butter with my bread!")

The Tiger Who Came to Tea by Judith Kerr has all the classic features: a setting familiar to children (mother and child, Sophie, about to have tea), an exotic addition in the form of a tiger who arrives ringing the doorbell, beautiful economy of language, with the much-loved list ("He ate all the buns on the dish . . . all the biscuits, and all the cake . . . And [he] drank all the milk in the jug, and all the

61

tea in the teapot . . . and all the orange juice, and all Daddy's beer, and all the water in the tap"). A vicarious delight in the misdeeds of others seems to characterise the reactions of most children from about three onwards; perhaps with an element of envy, as socially acceptable behaviour is increasingly expected from them? Even Cushla, unused to prohibitions, seemed to realise that *this* tiger's conduct was outrageous! But he was engaging, and very polite, and Sophie was utterly captivated. There are wonderful pictures of her sitting adoringly at his feet, gazing up at him, and lovingly draping his tail round her neck as he pursues his excesses.

Ultimately all is consumed and the tiger departs. Later Sophie and her bemused but unjudging parents go out "in the dark" (a continuing preoccupation) to a café and have "a lovely supper, with sausages and chips and ice-cream". Cushla, who cared not for food at all and could not be induced to try ice-cream, would gaze at this superbly executed picture of family indulgence tirelessly; and 'café' became one of her favourite words, a visit to one her constantly reiterated suggestion. The pictures in this book are uniquely uncluttered; only the essential is represented, against a white background, and everything mentioned is pictured, each illustration faithfully following the brief text. The use of colour is restrained but effective. It has that within-the-lines quality which has always seemed to aid Cushla's visual processes.

Cushla once more demonstrated, on this book, her willingness to accept that a pictured object may be imagined rather than real. When the bell rings, Sophie's mother speculates, "It can't be the milkman, because he came this morning . . . And it can't be Daddy . . ." Each possibility is pictured, and one is reminded of Dorothy White's description of *The Indoor Noisy Book*, which includes a series of questions: "Who is coming up the stairs? Is it a sailor, is it a soldier?" It is neither, but they too are pictured, and Carol, at two years eight months, contradicted her mother – "Yes it is, there he is" – and would not be dissuaded. Dorothy White suggests that, if the object exists only in the imagination of one of the characters, it should not be pictured, and, as a corollary, theorises, "If for a child what is in a picture is, likewise, what is not in a picture is not". She describes again Carol's refusal to accept that part of a person or thing existed if it were not pictured (citing the example of a mother who "stops at the waist" and of whom Carol asked, "Where is that mummy's head?") Carol was still demonstrating perplexity on this issue when over three years old (14 November 1948), while Cushla, 'reading' *The Tiger Who Came to Tea*, seemed clearly to understand that it was "*Not* the milkman, *not* Daddy . . ." despite their occurring as illustrations.

The genus tiger achieved a popularity at this time that has never waned. Each tiger encountered by *Little Black Sambo* (also introduced at this time) proposed to eat him up, until he offered, one by one, his beautiful little red coat, his blue trousers, his green umbrella, and his "lovely little pair of purple shoes, with crimson soles and crimson linings", but Cushla loved them nonetheless. She joyfully turned up the page in *At the Zoo* which depicts tigers, found several more in *Who Are We?* and used again and again phrases from the stories: "big, furry, stripy tiger" from *The Tiger Who Came to Tea* and "Now I'm the grandest tiger in the jungle!" from *Little Black Sambo*. Cushla was never frightened by this book, though it is often judged as too fearsome for a three-year-old. Perhaps, as Dorothy White suggests, Little Black Sambo's decisive placement, at the beginning of the story, in a secure family setting makes the difference, for Carol showed "no terror as she listened" either.

Several other books, introduced by reason of their real-story value, grew to be firm favourites. *Mr Gumpy's Motor Car* by John Burningham is that rare achievement, a completely successful sequel. The children and animals who insist upon sharing Mr Gumpy's car ride are just as cheerfully irresponsible as they appeared in the first book, Mr Gumpy himself just as unrufflable and accepting. All is well, in the end, Mr Gumpy once more inviting them all home, this time to swim in his pond. There is a lovely onomatopoeic string of verbs describing the car's progress to the top of the hill. Cushla learned it by heart, and several times produced it, rearranged for the occasion, as their own car toiled up the steep hill from Karekare to the main road ". . . strained, heaved, gasped, slipped, slithered, squelched, and edged its way to the top of the hill". A good example

63

of Dorothy White's "backward and forward flow between books and life".

Harry the Dirty Dog, Springtime for Jeanne-Marie, The Little Red Hen, and *The Three Billy Goats Gruff* all have the qualities of action and anticipation of climax which, when conveyed by an economically tuned text and pictures which have a worth of their own, and yet follow – even interpret – the text, speak directly to the three-year-old. In March 1975 each of these was read dozens of times. *Jeanne-Marie* was so high on the list as Cushla's operation approached that her mother had soft-toy models of the main characters, Jeanne-Marie, Jean-Pierre, the lamb Patapon, and the duck Madelon, made for Cushla's use in the hospital.

The honour of greatest impact, however, went in this month to *The Three Billy Goats Gruff.* Here is her mother's report dated 23 March 1975:

Read C. Paul Galdone's new book *The Three Billy Goats Gruff* for the first time this morning. Gave her usual attention, without comment; seemed rather worried. Later in day picked it up, settled herself and read as follows:

'This book 'bout billy goat. Look Mummy, there troll' (holding up book, showing M. full-page picture of troll, and laughing). 'Troll fall in water, troll make big loud noise. Me find troll. Troll make me fright. Troll like something to play with' (giving troll toy rabbit). 'Oooo! Troll likes it! Troll gave me terrible fright. Troll say "Roa-oar!" Oo-oo, see what happens – goat bump troll! Oo-oo, gave me terrible fright. See what happens? Troll stand on head in water. Billy goat go up hill, see 'nother billy goat. Like 'Tricia (M.) buy me troll at shop. Please write troll's name' (noticing M. writing). 'Me take troll's eye out' (picking at page). 'Troll fall splash plonk in water. Troll got drowned'.

Note that Cushla had listened to this book once only (five hours previously on same day). Although she had mastered 'troll' and 'billy goat', she had not memorised phrases. But she had absorbed some of

CUSHLA AND HER BOOKS

b

(Plate I)
B IS FOR BEAR by Dick Bruna
First used at 8 to 9 months.

Cushla formed a strong attachment to this book. The single letter on
each left-hand page obviously fascinated her. She would first gaze
intently at it, then move her eyes with great deliberation over to the
picture on the opposite page.

This is the dog,

(*Plate II*)
THE HOUSE THAT JACK BUILT by Rodney Peppé
First used at 8 to 9 months.

The repetitive flow seemed to be soothing to Cushla.

That worried the cat,
That killed the rat,
That ate the malt
That lay in the house
 that Jack built.

(*Plate III*)
BUT WHERE IS THE GREEN PARROT? by Thomas
and Wanda Zacharias
First used between 9 and 18 months.

Cushla had to have help the first time; thereafter she scanned each
picture carefully, finding the parrot with great satisfaction.

THE GARDEN
has a big tree
heavy with red apples,
a boat
sailing in a birdbath,
a watering can
for the yellow flowers —
BUT WHERE IS THE GREEN PARROT?

Papa and Mama Small buy groceries.

(Plate IV)
PAPA SMALL by Lois Lenski
First introduced between 9 and 18 months.

Lenski's square little characters may seem
unimaginative to adults, and their activities mundane,
but they enable the young child to see, perhaps for the
first time, that life goes on between the covers of a book.

The small Smalls help.

(Plate V)
HARRY THE DIRTY DOG by Gene Zion, illustrated
by Margaret Bloy Graham
First used between 18 months and 3 years.

A pet dog who gets so dirty that he changes from 'a white
dog with black spots to a black dog with white spots' is
totally comprehensible . . .

(Plate VI)
GRANDMOTHER LUCY AND HER HATS by Joyce Wood
illustrated by Frank Francis
First used between 18 months and 3 years.

This book perhaps served two purposes for Cushla, its homely detail confirmin
her own experience . . . and the touch of glamour in Grandmother Lucy's
succession of hats extending and expanding that experience.

Grandmother Lucy was a very,
very old Grandmother and she lived in
a house with red roses. The sun shone
on her red roses in the mornings.

When I went to see her, I knocked
at her door. The door was thick and
squeaked, and she always said, ''We must
oil the hinges.'' We never did, so it
squeaked and she smiled and I went in.

(Plate VII)
SHAWN GOES TO SCHOOL by Petronella Breinburg,
illustrated by Errol Lloyd
First used between 18 months and 3 years.

Cushla solicitously kissed his howling little face at every
reading. . . . Her identification with Sean was complete.

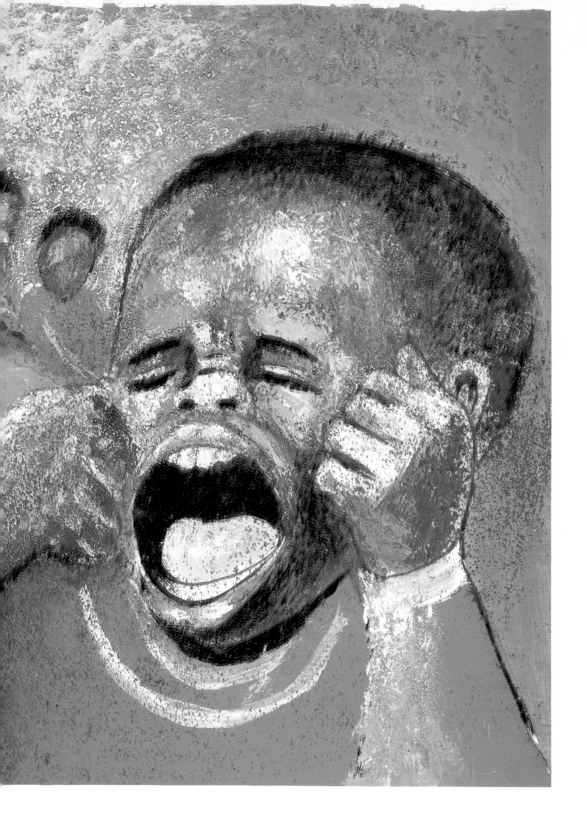

Most days Emma brushes her hair until it is smooth, and shines like silk.

(Plate VIII)
THIS IS BETSY by Gunilla Wolde
First used between 18 months and 3 years.

'I'm not Cushla, I'm Emma, and Emma roughs up her hair till she looks like a shaggy dog!'

But Emma quite contrary roughs up her hair
with her fingers until she looks like
a shaggy dog.

(Plate IX)
SPRINGTIME FOR JEANNE-MARIE by Françoise
First used between 3 years and 3 years, 3 months.

An economically tuned text and pictures which have a worth of their
own and yet follow – even interpret – the text! . .

Sophie opened
the door, and
there was a big,
furry,
stripy tiger.
The tiger said,
"Excuse me, but
I'm very hungry.
Do you think
I could have
tea with you?"
Sophie's Mummy
said, "Of course,
come in."

(Plate X)
THE TIGER WHO CAME TO TEA by Judith Kerr
First used between 3 years and 3 years, 3 months.

The pictures are uniquely uncluttered; only the essential is represented
against a white background, and everything mentioned is pictured . . .

So the tiger came into the kitchen and sat down at the table.

They each had a bowl for their porridge.

The Little Wee Bear
had a little wee bowl,

the Middle-Sized Bear
had a middle-sized bowl,

and the Great Big Bear
had a great big bowl.

(Plate XI)
THE THREE BEARS by Paul Galdone
First used between 3 years and 3 years, 3 months.

The animals are huge and lumbering; real bears, not
dressed up humans . . .

They each had a chair to sit in.

The Little Wee Bear
had a little wee chair,

the Middle-Sized Bear
had a middle-sized chair,

and the Great Big Bear
had a great big chair.

(Plate XII)
THE THREE BILLY GOATS GRUFF by Paul Galdone
First used between 3 years and 3 years, 3 months.

The impact is eloquent. The troll himself is almost all
head, with fuzzy hair setting off features at once
malevolent and roguish.

But on the way up there was
a bridge over a rushing river.
And under the bridge lived a Troll
who was as fierce as he was ugly.

(Plate XIII)
THE ELEPHANT AND THE BAD BABY by Elfrida Vipont,
illustrated by Raymond Briggs
First used between 3 years, 3 months and 3 years, 9
months.

Energetic pictures and a memorable repeated line 'and
they went rumpeta, rumpeta, rumpeta all down the road'
ensures its endurance . . .

So the Elephant stretched out his trunk, and picked up the Bad Baby and put him on his back, and they went rumpeta, rumpeta, rumpeta, all down the road, with the ice-cream man, and the pork butcher, and the baker, and the snack bar man, and the grocer, and the lady from the sweet shop, and the barrow boy all running after.

He took his axe
and cut the cat open.
And out jumped
the parson with the crooked staff
and the lady with the pink parasol

(*Plate XIV*)
THE FAT CAT by Jack Kent
First used between 3 years, 3 months and 3 years, 9 months.

This ribald tale was presented to Cushla as a jest and
accepted as such. For good measure, two of the victims
are called Skohottentot and Skolinkenlot.

and the seven girls dancing
and the five birds in a flock
and Skolinkenlot
and Skohottentot.

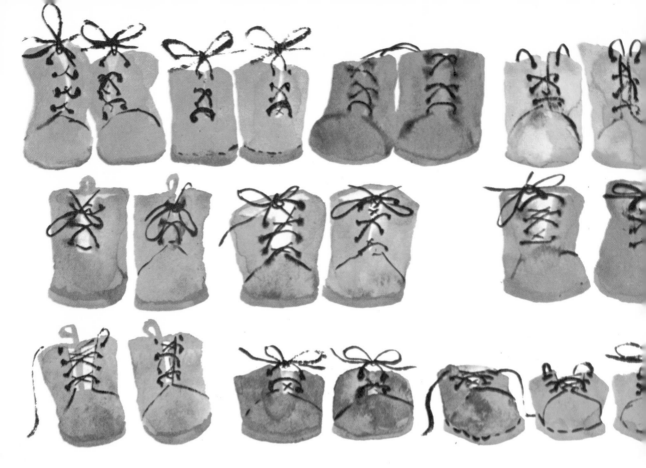

what he cut out at night was finished in the mornir
so that he was soon again in comfortable circumstar
and became a well-to-do man.

(*Plate XV*)
THE ELVES AND THE SHOEMAKER from Grimm,
retold by Katrin Brandt
First used between 3 years, 3 months and 3 years, 9 months.

It is hard to believe that a double-page spread containing
thirty pairs of different-sized laced boots (plus an odd
one) could exert such fascination.

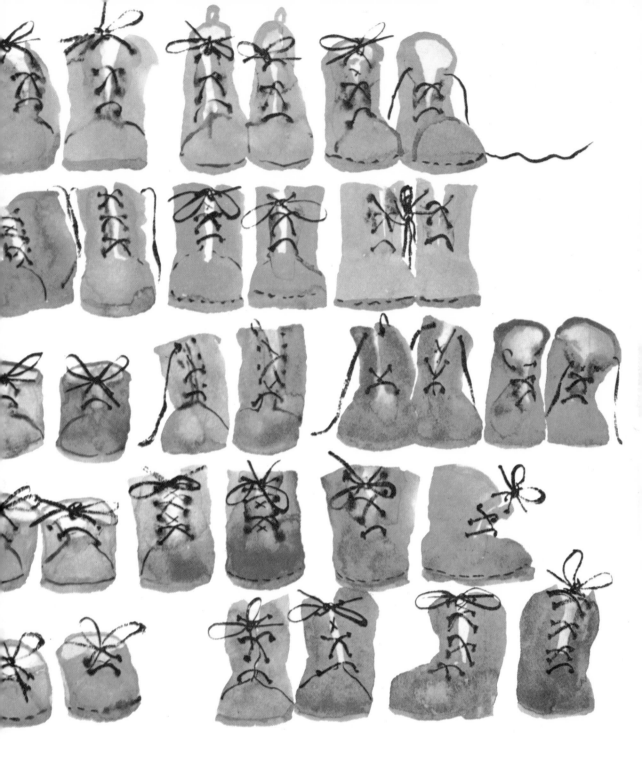

(Plate XVI, overleaf)
THE LITTLE WOODEN FARMER by Alice Dalgleish,
illustrated by Anita Lobel
First used between 3 years, 3 months and 3 years, 9 months.

No book has ever been more loved by Cushla than this
one. Its appeal must surely be to all three-year-olds, for
its features are classic.

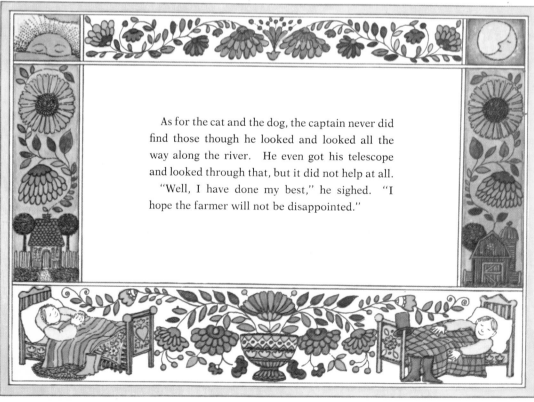

As for the cat and the dog, the captain never did find those though he looked and looked all the way along the river. He even got his telescope and looked through that, but it did not help at all.

"Well, I have done my best," he sighed. "I hope the farmer will not be disappointed."

the essence of the story, including its frightening nature. She seems to have loved the word 'troll' and to have found him simultaneously frightening and likeable; she mentioned him no fewer than fifteen times in the reported reading, almost as if she found the word itself enjoyable, quite apart from her obvious fascination with the idea. (At Easter, late in the month, Cushla's cat was discovered eating one of her Easter eggs. 'You naughty old troll-pussy!' said Cushla with feeling.)

Her mother's diary concludes:

> At night both her father and I read the story to C. again, at her request, and she seemed greatly excited by the troll, clasping her hands in front of her body and kicking her legs with the thrill of it. Almost as if she enjoys being frightened!

In this book, Galdone has used much the same technique as he employed in his other 'new' retelling *The Three Bears*, mentioned later in this section. The views of the billy goats mounting the bridge are breathtaking in their stark drama; he uses the area provided by a double-page spread of very large pages (in all, 44 cm × 28 cm), and the impact is eloquent. The troll himself is almost all head, with fuzzy hair setting off features at once malevolent and roguish. Cushla played being the troll (never one of the goats) with riotous enjoyment, always leaping from under the table to which she had assigned the role of bridge and shouting "Now I'm going to eat you up!" long before the appropriate moment in the story arrived.

This period saw, also, an upsurge in Cushla's enjoyment of the absurd in books. Sparked off by *Emma Quite Contrary* by Gunilla Wolde, it extended to include *I Don't Want To, Said Sara* by Hans Peterson, which was provided to add fuel to the new fire. In both books small girls perform ludicrous and unlikely acts. Emma's background is the here and now, but Sara escapes from the world of reality on the end of a magic rope. " 'Let go of the rope!' cried Mother. 'I don't want to,' said Sara. And she flew away."

Emma puts her pants on her head, and Cushla shrieked with laughter and copied her example next morning. 'Just like dumb old

65

Emma,' she said, using a phrase which she had picked up from other children at Play Centre, and was using with relish. Emma made a marked impression upon Cushla, and five months later was still cropping up constantly in her conversation. 'Emma doesn't like contrary blocks, she kicks them if they fall down' was overheard one day as her own ineptly built structure collapsed and she followed Emma's example. 'Doesn't Cushla like contrary blocks either?' asked her mother. 'I'm not Cushla, I'm Emma and Emma roughs up her hair 'til she looks like a shaggy dog!' said Cushla with feeling, wildly ruffling her own.

The distinctive feature of these books and of *Mog, the Forgetful Cat* by Judith Kerr, is their nonsensical quality; the three-year-old demands a note of slapstick in his comedy and, indeed, is unimpressed by subtlety.

In the field of number and counting books, Bruna's *I Can Count* was joined by Clare Bowes' *How Many?*, an indigenous book featuring animals and objects peculiar to New Zealand: "two tuataras, six nikau palms, three tuis". Cushla's parents had ascertained, with the help of blocks, that she had an understanding of 'three' at this stage; she could isolate one, two, or three blocks and could count objects in a one-to-one correspondence up to three. This is average for a three-year-old. Another facet of Cushla's sense of humour was demonstrated during this month by her recourse to these two counting books. One day, when listening to *I Can Count* (which she had requested), she snatched the book from her mother at "six socks", shouted with gusto, 'No! Six nikau palms!' and laughed delightedly. She showed the picture to several people present, repeating 'Six nikau palms' and obviously expecting them to laugh, which they obligingly did. Next morning she asked for *How Many?* and at "six nikau palms" laughed and said, 'See? See?' obviously recalling yesterday's joke.

Cushla's sense of size-relationship enjoyed an apparent boost at this time from contact with Paul Galdone's *The Three Bears*, a new retelling of the traditional story in which the animals are huge and lumbering; real bears, not dressed-up humans. The book itself is big (26 cm × 26 cm) and the little girl untraditionally homely. "Little wee, middle-sized and great big" offered Cushla new opportunities for classification, and for a few weeks the opportunity was explored to its limit. Her own toes, weights from the kitchen scales, loaves of bread and sand castles were all subjected to the system, and it was clear that she had grasped the principle. One day she took *Little, Big, Bigger*, a book that she had neglected for many months, from the bookshelves and began to read it. First came "A little elephant, a big elephant, a bigger elephant"; then she applied the new process; "A little wee house, a middle-sized house, a great big house" for the rest of the book.

There was increasing and welcome evidence at this time that Cushla was at last drawing from the world around her instead of relying on direct 'teaching', as seemed the case earlier. On finding a pocket diary, she turned successive pages. 'This Monday, this Tuesday'. And then, finding a map at the end, 'Go round here, down there', tracing a path with her finger. She also seemed to realise suddenly that one could buy almost anything from a shop. This led to some surprising requests. 'Please buy me a dinosaur'! (from *What is Big?* by Wing). Her language, although explicit, was rather staccato; articles, conjunctions, and parts of the verb 'to be' were frequently omitted, and just as often, an incorrect verb form would be used. After lining up blue pegs on her pegboard, she said, 'Me make blue road. Sophie go down blue road to café', which correctly spoken, would become '*I am making a* blue road. Sophie *goes* down *the* blue road to *a* café'. In two sentences, that is, Cushla used the first pronoun singular in the wrong case, two verbs in the wrong form and omitted two indefinite and one definite articles. And yet the utterance revealed both knowledge, imagination and memory. (In *The Tiger Who Came to Tea* Sophie and her parents "walked down the road to a café".)

One is led to wonder whether, perhaps, Cushla was not still producing a high proportion of 'contentives' (words carrying semantic content – usually nouns, adjectives and adverbs) (Brown and Bellagi 1964) and whether, also, this might not indicate that her speech development was dependent to a greater than usual degree upon imitation.

Cushla and her books

Cushla at this time spent considerable, and increasingly lengthy, periods 'reading' aloud to herself from her books. There was no doubt that she had developed a retentive memory. Her mother's report for Thursday 20 March notes:

C. read to herself for forty minutes again today. Books in this order:
  Emma Quite Contrary
  Springtime for Jeanne-Marie
  Me and My Flying Machine
  The Lazy Bear
  Mr Gumpy's Outing
  Mr Gumpy's Motor Car.
All word perfect, making some allowance for slurring over sentences.

She also knew by heart many songs and rhymes, which she sang or repeated constantly while playing. Her mother listed those heard most frequently during March:

Here we go Looby Lou
Ring-a-Ring o' Roses
Twinkle Twinkle Little Star
Hush Little Baby
The North Wind Doth Blow
Rock-a-bye Baby
Baa-baa Black Sheep
Down by the Station
This Old Man, he Played 'One'
Figgy Pudding (family version of Christmas carol).

And she had committed to memory almost every poem in Milne's *When We Were Very Young*. Another collection, *The Young Puffin Book of Verse* had been introduced several months before and was now entrenched among the favourites. Compiled by Barbara Ireson, this book is notable for the perception that has been used in the

68

choice of poems. Too often, in such a volume, the level is inconsistent; here, one can use every poem with assurance. Cushla was delighted to find several of her Milne favourites in the new book, and earnestly turned up the originals for comparison.

There seemed to be no doubt that the rhyme and the rhythm of these poems had sensory appeal for Cushla; one was forced to recognise this in her unfailing response to Milne's 'The Island', a poem which could not possibly have evoked for her a recognisable image.

She would listen with glazed eyes, obviously, unquestionably, intoxicated with words.

> Up, up, up, staggering stumbling,
> Round the corner where the rock is crumbling,
> Round this shoulder,
> Over this boulder,
> Up to the top where the six trees stand . . .

Cushla knows this poem by heart, and repeats it, all three verses and concluding couplet, and one is reminded of Eve Merriam's injunction in 'How to Eat a Poem':

> Don't be polite.
> Bite in
> Pick it up with your fingers and lick the juice
> that may run down your chin . . .
> For there is no core
> or stem
> or rind
> or pit
> or seed
> or skin
> to throw away.

All of this material had, of course, been 'taught' to Cushla. There can be no way of estimating the extent to which her rote learning of such material had assisted her in the internalisation of speech, with consequent generation of language.

Cazden (1968), discussing the child's acquisition of language, says:

> In contrast to variety are well-learned routines. These may include sentences such as 'I don't know'. They may also include bits of nursery rhymes and songs, and, perhaps most important of all, phrases from books read to the child many times. It has been a long time since Carroll (1939) suggested, 'An interesting investigation could be set upon the hypothesis that learning of rote material is an important factor in speech development.' That investigation still remains to be done.

In 1975, it still remains to be done. Only the existence of a similarly afflicted child, acting as control, and not receiving the book-stimulation to which Cushla was exposed, could have facilitated an experiment casting possible light on the effectiveness of this stimulation to compensate for handicapping features, and no such child was, or could have been, available. In fact, of course, Cushla's 'treatment' was not seen as such by her parents. It was simply their way of enriching her life, a life which might, in other circumstances, have been impoverished.

This month has been reproduced in some detail as it constituted, for Cushla, something of an oasis.

No part of her earlier life had had the undisturbed quality of this short period. No infections or emergencies arose to interfere with the peace of the long days, and her parents' delight at her progress, their joy in the new baby's healthy growth and their conviction that the move to Karekare had been beneficial to the whole family, pervaded both children's lives.

The intensification of her mother's recording had an unforeseen side-effect; Cushla became very interested in 'writing' and frequently asked her mother to 'write my name', 'write Daddy's name' and so on. Before long, a game developed in which the Christian name of each member of the family was written down, Cushla then pointing to each in turn and saying it. She already knew the capitals C. for Cushla, P. for Patricia, etc, and this no doubt helped identification. However, she quickly learned to distinguish between 'Sanchia' and 'Stephen', despite the identical initial. Her mother's entry of 10 March notes that:

> C. is very interested in writing names and words. Holds pencil in near-normal grip, but with first finger crooked round it. Has started making small, careful marks instead of large sweeping scrawls. But so far unintelligible – C. translates for us.

Later in the month she wrote:

> Cushla now makes shaky 'C's' (for Cushla) everywhere – on paper and in the sand. Not often the right way up.

It was quite apparent at the same time that Cushla knew that the text in a book carried the language. Often, she would 'read aloud' from an adult book which had no pictures.

Her identification of colours had been consolidated over the preceding few months; informal 'testing' in late March revealed that she was sure of all the basic colours, and had added purple without specific teaching.

Cushla's lack of co-ordination in arm, hand and finger manipulation was still seen in her inability to assemble jigsaw puzzles of any complexity. One constantly had the feeling that she knew the area in which a piece belonged, but that the relative clumsiness of her fingers prevented her from experimentation with the pieces. A procedure whereby an adult 'helped' with the task did, however, allow her some experience with manipulative material.

One of Cushla's strongest features, in the context of her physical handicaps, has always been her lack of frustrated or angry reaction to her own incapacity. She has always given up cheerfully after an honest attempt. This was (and still is) her attitude to intricate puzzles.

There could be no doubt that Cushla had made steady progress since her last assessment at two years, nine months. Her language use had expanded markedly in terms of both semantic content and syntactic structure. She was showing interest in identifying and writing capital letters, and could now 'read aloud' from a wide range of books, matching text to picture. She was using words from books read to her in new, correct contexts, and gave evidence of ability to draw inference from material read ('Can't smell *that* fire, only our fire in there', pointing to fireplace, on encountering a bonfire in *Smells I Like*).

Emotionally, she was coping with the inroads of an energetic seven-months-old sister into her parents' time and attention; physically, she was discovering, as all first children must, that one's books can be torn and one's toys moved or even broken in the cause of the newcomer's experimentation. Cushla was taking these things in her stride.

Physically, she had never been as well. Her parents' realisation that this probably indicated the approach of the long-planned kidney operation did little to lessen their pleasure in her progress. Life for Cushla, and for them, was assuming a new quality, and this was enjoyed to the full.

Chapter Six

THREE YEARS, THREE MONTHS TO
THREE YEARS, NINE MONTHS

In March 1975, at a routine check at Auckland Hospital, the paediatrician in charge of Cushla's case announced her intention of consulting the kidney specialist, with a view to repairing or removing Cushla's left kidney.

The possibility of extension of infection to the other kidney, or other organs, was always present; only Cushla's ill health and frail condition had prevented operation earlier.

Extensive tests were carried out during April to ascertain that Cushla was, indeed, strong enough to face the operation, and Cushla responded to these with cheerful acceptance. Her parents attempted to prepare her for what was to come, with the result that she talked about 'going to the hospital and sleeping there' and told friends that 'the doctor's going to fix up my tummy'.

Her mother's diary of 30 April says '. . . at the hospital most of the day having tests. C. very co-operative and quite happy to be there.'

At her parents' insistence, and with the co-operation of the hospital authorities (who now accepted their firm views on this subject), arrangements were made for Cushla's family to 'room in'. For the ten days that Cushla was in hospital, her father slept each night in her room. Her mother, with the baby (now eight months old), stayed with friends who lived near the hospital, and came in each morning. For the first few days, the parents would change places during the day. After this period, when Cushla was no longer ill, it proved quite possible for the family, mother, father, and two children, to spend the day together. Cushla's grandmother relieved the parents each day in the early afternoon, allowing them to have a break with the younger child. During Cushla's last few days in hospital the weather was fine, and the family spent enjoyable periods in the Auckland Domain, with Cushla in a wheelchair and Sanchia in her pushchair.

It proved possible to repair the kidney, and this was done. As described earlier (Chapter One) hydronephrosis of the kidney is a condition in which the funnel-shaped outlet is so enlarged that X-ray cannot determine the state of the kidney proper. The operation revealed a normal-sized kidney, and the decision was made on the spot to remove the excess tissue, construct a normal outlet and endeavour to persuade the kidney to take over its normal half-share of disposal of body waste.

More than usual difficulty attended the procedure. In order to inspect the spleen and other organs, the surgeon had decided to approach from the front, rather than make the usual entry through the back. Repair and reconstruction was a more delicate technique than removal, and the avenue of approach increased the difficulty.

Several anxious days followed the operation until it was established that the repaired kidney was taking over its share of work. During this time, Cushla seemed to be surrounded by bottles – a saline drip into her arm, one bottle into which blood and other matter dripped, and a third (from which she was parted only one day before discharge) which collected urine, to be measured against that processed by the normal kidney and passed naturally, until each amount should be equal.

Cushla acquitted herself admirably through these tense days, co-operating in all ways, and showing an extraordinary grasp of the situation. She may not have known why such an unpleasant performance was necessary, but she clearly accepted that it was. Doctors and nurses alike remarked upon her tolerance of procedures that were trying and often painful; she cautioned visitors to 'mind my bottles!' and quickly learned that it was worth requesting that a thermometer be placed under her arm rather than in her mouth.

Cushla emerged from the hospital six pounds lighter. In appearance she was thin and pale, but the repaired kidney was working well, and no complications had arisen.

During each of the three previous winters of her life, Cushla had been subjected to emergency hospitalisation as her physical condition deteriorated to an alarming level. The winter of 1975 struck a new note of hope; Cushla, although afflicted in turn with an ear infection, a cold and a bout of tonsillitis, weathered all three, with recourse only to the help of the family doctor, at home. Convulsions associated with a high temperature in June led to the prescribing of phenobarbitone, to be kept on hand for such emergencies.

A month after her operation, she was able to begin weekly swimming lessons at the Crippled Children's Society's pool, and, despite some time lost through illness, made excellent progress. Her earlier confidence continued, and a summer spent at Karekare where a freshwater stream, augmented each tide by incoming salt water, forms an ideal swimming pool for small children, further helped her progress. It was noted in January that her prowess in the water was superior to that of other children of her age.

A large pedal tricycle was acquired in August, and Cushla mastered the art of riding it, although she still used her small 'hobby-horse' tricycle more often. The large one gained in popularity as Cushla grew in height and strength – the smaller one, in the meanwhile, was clearly more fun.

Cushla's ability to run about and play had increased greatly during the year. She was now walking long distances on the firm sand of the beach, scrambling up sandhills, climbing, and generally following the active life that characterises the three-year-old. She was still easily knocked over, and her arms were very weak, but, by and large, she was able to pursue a normal child's activities. Waiatarua Play Centre (which the family had joined early in the year) was helping to meet Cushla's needs for companionship, and a younger boy who also lived in Karekare played with her almost daily.

Cushla's eye-hand co-ordination was improving, although slowly. She still found intricate puzzles too difficult, and needed help with dressing (considerably more than the average child, according to Gesell norms). She could now paint, using a separate large brush for each colour and returning each brush to its jar. The result was often recognisably a figure or object, which she would label verbally. She had also, after much practice, mastered the use of scissors and 'cutting out' was added to her occupations.

Cushla and her books

At three years, eight months, Cushla learned to jump (on the spot) with two feet together. This was a clumsy performance, but involved some concentration and effort, and obviously gave her great satisfaction. She never tired of demonstrating; one was reminded of hand-clapping, two years before, and the great joy its mastery had given her.

Cushla's use of books was now divided almost equally between 'reading' aloud herself from her books, and being read to by adults. She had fallen into a pattern of coming into her parents' bed early in the morning, and they soon saw the wisdom of keeping a pile of books at hand. Cushla would 'read aloud', often for over an hour, only involving one of them if the book was a new one and she needed help.

A very large number of new books were introduced during this period. Only those which made a marked impact on Cushla can be mentioned in the text, although all are listed in Appendix B (p. 112).

Cushla's enjoyment of the ridiculous became even more marked at this time. *My Cat Likes to Hide in Boxes* by a New Zealander, Eve Sutton, was soon committed to memory, to be performed on innumerable occasions with great hilarity. The book uses rhymed couplets, beginning with:

> The cat from France
> Likes to sing and dance –
> But My Cat likes to hide in boxes

adding another couplet at every opening. They are all nonsensical, and a wonderful list of unlikely lunacies is cumulatively built up. Predictably, "the cat from Norway got stuck in the doorway" passed into Cushla's everyday language. The illustrations, in line, are unremarkable but adequate. It is the text that distinguishes this book. It has rhythm, rhyme, repetition and invention; one's faith in the natural humour and the sure ear of the human child is bolstered when language, rather than bright colours, carries the day.

The Fat Cat, an old Danish folk-tale retold and illustrated with verve and originality by Jack Kent, might be supposed to terrify a young child, with its saga of victims to its hero's gluttony: not only "the gruel, and the pot, and the old woman too" but an impressive list of luckless innocents before the tale is all but told – by which time the outrageous animal is so fat (he fills a whole page, almost) that something has to happen. . . . The sight of "the parson with the crooked staff, and the lady with the pink parasol, and the seven girls dancing . . ." all scuttling safely home, is excelled only by the poor little cat himself, on the last page, sticking-plaster applied to his middle. The kindly woodcutter, who had seen his duty clear, tends him solicitously. This ribald tale was presented to Cushla as a jest and accepted as such. For good measure, two of the victims are called Skohottentot and Skolinkenlot, and there is a marvellous, regularly repeated line which Cushla added to a growing list of 'threats' from her literature, "And now I am going to also eat YOU!"

Fish Out of Water, one of the earlier Collins Beginner Books by Helen Palmer, is a story of domestic carnage brought on by the overfeeding of a goldfish, Otto. During his catastrophic growth spurt, the house is almost wrecked, the police and the fire brigade called in, to no avail . . . excess piles upon excess. All is well in the end (a stern requirement for the pre-schooler), but meanwhile slapstick has its way. Cushla took to shrieking with laughter at these stories, flinging her legs in the air and hugging herself with joy.

Of quite different quality was her reaction to Barbara Macfarlane's *Naughty Agapanthus*, who joined Sara and Emma in their different protests at a world which demanded order and obedience. Agapanthus, ensconced in a virtuous family (even her baby brother is "mostly very good"), is sometimes VERY NAUGHTY! She runs outside, against firm instructions, in scanty underwear, swims in the fishpond, catches a terrible cold, and, when the doctor comes she shouts, to his polite request that she open her mouth, "I won't! I won't" and, when he persists, she bites his finger. "Yes, she bit the doctor's finger nearly to the bone!"

Cushla's enjoyment of this was of the hand-over-mouth, horrified-disbelief variety; one did not bite doctors! It is actually, in its way, a cautionary tale; Agapanthus refuses to take her "purple medicine . . .

77

but her mother tipped it in". She decides to be good. "Sure enough, when the doctor came, she opened her mouth most beautifully. 'Very fine tonsils' said the doctor. 'Tomorrow you may get up, if you wear a warm red jumper'."

There is no bulk in this text. The language is precise, beautifully tuned. The pictures by Margaret Lees have real virtuosity; in unlikely shades of pink, purple, orange and turquoise, with a cut-paper look, they somehow bring Agapanthus and her story alive. This is an unfailing book.

Traditional stories, first met in the persons of 'The Three Bears', 'The Three Billy Goats Gruff', and 'The Little Red Hen', came into their own at this time with the acquisition of *The Jack Kent Book of Nursery Tales*. This splendid volume contains seven of the simplest stories, including 'The Gingerbread Man', 'Little Red Riding Hood', 'The Three Little Pigs', and 'Chicken Licken'. These are very simple retellings, with three or four bright, explicit illustrations on each large page. Two other stories in the same collection, 'The Little Red Hen' and 'The Three Bears' provided the additional experience of meeting already familiar stories in a new version (an experience not new to Cushla, however – by this time she owned three versions of 'The Owl and the Pussycat').

The Contents page of this book is an enjoyable experience for a child; each story title and its page number is included as part of a fairy-tale house. Cushla pored over this bonus, as she does over the endpapers and title-pages of many of her books.

The Elves and the Shoemaker, a retelling from Grimm quite exquisitely illustrated by Katrin Brandt, also struck exactly the right note from its introduction. It is hard to believe that a double-page spread containing thirty pairs of different-sized laced boots (plus an odd one) in varying shades of yellowish reddish brown, could exert such fascination. These pictures have no background; people and objects are randomly placed – a pair of scissors, a spool of thread, the clothes that the shoemaker and his wife make for the elves, all laid out squarely for the child to identify and assign. And then here are the "little men", capering wildly (surely one of the most enchanting spreads ever produced) each in exactly the clothes that were earlier shown, an important requirement for the observant near-four-year-old.

(A very successful book, *Susan Cannot Sleep* by Kaj Beckman, illustrates this insistence on consistency in illustration. Susan's pillow has her name on it in three successive pictures, but it is missing in the next. 'Where's Susan's name gone?' asked Cushla. While her father looked baffled, she fortunately found an explanation herself. 'I know. She turned her pillow over!')

It would be easy to theorise that Cushla's enduring affection for books embodying the home-and-security theme reflected the number of upsets to her own security which her almost constant ill-health and, in particular, her recent operation had precipitated. In fact, there is little evidence for this proposition, and it has been impossible to isolate any harmful effect of her kidney operation. For the first two days, while she was ill and in pain, she wanted only to lie, with one or other of her parents reassuringly with her. Thereafter she sat up, read her books, talked, played with her toys, and generally joined in the life about her.

Once home, Cushla resumed her life without pause. A comparison with Carol White's life at this age reveals many likenesses – at least in the children's preoccupations. Both little girls seemed beset with domestic fervour. Dorothy White reports cleaning operations which rendered "the mimic housekeeper as tired as the real one", and Cushla's mother writes of her daughter, "She has a passion for clearing up and putting away. Says with satisfaction 'Now it's all tidy and clean'." Both children instruct and admonish their parents; in both cases their current reading shines through:

Carol: Don't go on the street cars, run over and get some buns, and don't go in Mr McGregor's garden.

Cushla: Well, please stay home and mind the house. I'm going shopping [to] buy fresh bread, baked beans and tarts from Grandmother's shop.

Both children met Wanda Gàg's *Millions of Cats* at this time, and both, as thousands of children before them (it was first published in 1929) fell under its spell, relishing the repeated lines "hundreds of cats, thousands of cats, millions and billions and trillions of cats" and committing them to memory. Cushla made "hundreds of spots, thousands of spots . . ." on her painting within a few days, and Carol saw "hundreds of cows . . . millions of cows" on a holiday soon after.

Both Carol and Cushla continued in their devotion to *Peter Rabbit*, Carol requesting the story each day, and asking endless questions about the detail in Beatrix Potter's stories, and Cushla drawing her mother's attention to a network of power lines overhead: 'that looks like a gooseberry net'. At her mother's baffled expression she laughed and said, 'Peter Rabbit got caught in a gooseberry net by brass buttons on jacket. It was a blue jacket, quite new'.

Dorothy White mentions Carol's increased enjoyment at this stage of several books which she had met at an earlier age, but which now had more relevance in the light of expanding experience. Of one of these she says ". . . since Carol last saw it, she had been attended by the doctor, had seen her own baby sister fed with a bottle, and had watched the spring-cleaning before we moved house". In much the same way, *Little Mummy*, *Helping at Home*, and another book describing a typical day in the lives of two pre-schoolers, *At Home* by L. A. Ivory, all enjoyed an upsurge of attention now that Cushla was at last able to 'help' make the beds, give milk to the cat, and work in the garden. Even a new copy of *Davy's Day* provided for Sanchia, as Cushla's old copy had been loved to death, was seized upon. Much as she had enjoyed him, Cushla had never before been able really to share Davy's activities.

Dorothy White echoes the perplexity of all who read to young children and speculate on the relative merits of different books, when she wonders ". . . how one should assess the comparative value of *The Little Family* [by Lois Lenski] and *Peter Rabbit*." She suspects ". . . that a child has a need both for the book which 'merely' confirms, like *The Little Family* and for the book like *Peter Rabbit* which extends beyond the immediately known". Twenty-seven years later, there seems nothing to add to that statement.

The Little Wooden Farmer by Alice Dalgliesh, with exquisite illustrations by Anita Lobel, came Cushla's way at this time. Published in 1930, it goes quietly on; an outstanding book which has never really achieved the fame it deserves. The Little Wooden Farmer and his wife have a delightful farm, but no animals. They enlist the captain of the steamboat which calls daily at their dock, and he promises to find them ". . . a brown cow that gives rich creamy milk, two white sheep with warm woolly coats, a fat pink pig with a curly tail, a rooster that will crow in the morning, a hen that will lay a large brown egg each day, a dog to guard the house and a cat to sit on the doorstep or purr by the fire".

Infinite attention to design has been given in this superb little book. The text is exactly and beautifully ensconced in a decorated frame; all the animals, human characters and a profusion of other small objects recur in an ornamented border over which the child will pore for hours. No book has ever been more loved by Cushla than this one. Its appeal must surely be to all three-year-olds, for its features are classic.

Cushla had had 'The Nutshell Library' since before she went into hospital. She never tired of packing and unpacking the four tiny books into their slip-cover, and loved all of Sendak's text – particularly *Pierre*, a cautionary tale whose hero has qualities in common with Emma, Sara and Agapanthus. Sendak's most famous book, *Where the Wild Things Are*, was also introduced at this time. This is a story which commonly excites apprehension in the breast of the adult proposing to introduce it. Will the young child be terrified by the monsters who "roar their terrible roars, and gnash their terrible teeth and roll their terrible eyes and show their terrible claws"? Experience shows that, provided the story is read with adult confidence, they are not; indeed they are enchanted. The secret seems to lie in the fact that Max, who "sails off through night and day and in and out of weeks and almost over a year to where the Wild Things are," is always in control. He tames them with his magic trick of "staring into all their yellow eyes . . ." and when he finally is ". . . sad and wants to be where someone loves him best of all" he leaves them, despite their pleas ("We'll eat you up, we love you so!") and returns home to his supper, which is "still hot".

81

Sendak's text is pure poetry; one could not voluntarily stop in the middle. It offers the child a literary experience, at the same time nourishing his imagination and providing him with a visual feast. The monsters are like nothing else encountered in literature; Sendak's three, whole, unlabelled spreads of "wild rumpus" excite and delight in equal proportions. Cushla was totally captivated.

The Elephant and the Bad Baby is a boisterous tale which starts with age-old simplicity: "Once upon a time there was an Elephant. And one day the Elephant went for a walk and he met a Bad Baby . . ." Enlivened by Raymond Briggs's energetic pictures, the story grows – and a memorable, repeated line, "and they went rumpeta, rumpeta, rumpeta all down the road", ensures its endurance in the memory of the fortunate listener.

Many other books – *Corduroy, The Cow Who Fell in the Canal, Go Tell Aunt Rhody, The Wind Blew, The Terrible Tiger, Farmer Barnes and Bluebell* and many others – played their parts, and continued in daily use.

Cushla's father now takes her and her small sister in once weekly to the Te Atatu library, and Cushla is learning to borrow books, as well as to own them. Occasional fits of stubbornness are expected, and accepted; the only book which to date has had to be bought for Cushla before she would agree to return the library copy is Sendak's *In the Night Kitchen* – although there is currently room for apprehension in her devotion to the Roses' *How Saint Francis Tamed the Wolf*!

The period just described witnessed a remarkable increase in Cushla's command of language. In March, at three years, three months, she was still using 'me' as the subject of a sentence, and using simple sentences (unless quoting direct from a book). Now, less than six months later, she was using the correct pronoun form 'I', complex sentence forms, reporting other people's speech, using past and future tenses, and the subjunctive ('Clive might take a photo of Sanchia').

Surprisingly, her period in hospital seemed to coincide with an acceleration in her speech and understanding generally. Compare her comments before entering hospital (p. 73) with this entry in her mother's report, dated 31 May: "'When I was at hospital last morning the doctor say he got a brand new hospital, he did. What I say Mum? I say I got a brand new beach!' (laughed)."

In this utterance, Cushla reported an exchange between herself and the doctor, in the course of which she had held her own, apparently! ('Brand new beach' presumably referred to the move to Karekare.)

Several months later, bringing her father a book, she said, 'Vivi gave this me one day when she was home and she said "Here you are Cushla, this a book I had when I a little girl and now I think I give it to you," she said'. The speech of three-year-old children is widely different, depending on features inherent and environmental; but there can be no doubt that Cushla's speech was enabling her to represent the world, express her thoughts, report occurrences and reflect on possibilities – in short, to communicate.

Perhaps the most joyous of her mother's entries was that dated 22 August, just before this study closed:

Spent the day in town. To swimming in the morning, then to visit Trudy, then Lisa and Steven (small friends) then to Grannie's. Only had one book all day . . . I almost never need to read to Cushla when we spend the day in town. She is so excited to see her friends that she never comes near me or asks for a book. She is too busy playing rowdy games.

Cushla was tested on the Stanford-Binet Intelligence Scale (Form L-M) on 1 August 1975, at the age of three years, eight months. The psychologist's report is here reproduced in full.

INTELLIGENCE

Assessed on the Stanford-Binet Intelligence Scale (Form L-M), Cushla performed at above average, IQ range being 104–114. Again, she was most co-operative, though tired, and her mother assisted on occasions. She passed all tests save opposite analogies at the four-year-old level, and four tests at the four-and-a-half-year-old level – tests unrelated to a visual image and those involving finer motor movements are difficult as yet.

ATTAINMENT

Cushla 'read' two picture books at the end of the interview with accuracy and enthusiasm, these being only two of the many with which she is conversant. All the pre-reading skills appear well established. There seemed to be from time to time some slight difficulty in eye focusing.

PERSONAL ADJUSTMENT AND BEHAVIOUR

Cushla is a happy, relaxed child equally at home with adults and peers.

CONCLUSIONS AND RECOMMENDATIONS

Cushla has made remarkable progress over the period of time since she has been receiving assessment, but in particular over the last twelve months. It is possible that the change to living in a 'country' area has helped in assisting her to sleep for longer periods and in building up her general health. Thanks to parental care her period in hospital has caused no break in development, no cause for future separation problems.

It would be useful to have her eyes checked if this has not already been planned for, and to arrange for as much interaction with other children as is possible having regard to health and geographic situation.

Progress should be reviewed before her fifth birthday.

It seems hardly necessary to add anything to these results. As they stand, they describe Cushla very well indeed.

There seems every likelihood, discounting unforeseen difficulties, that Cushla's progress will continue. The fact that tests 'unrelated to a visual image and involving finer motor movements are difficult at the moment' indicates that, as Cushla herself learns progressively to cope with her handicaps, an improvement in score will result.

As is noted, Cushla was tired at the time of testing; leaving home early in the morning, she had had a swimming lesson and been to visit a friend before being tested in early afternoon. That she was still happy, relaxed and co-operative reflects her developing attitudes to people and situations. She is ordinarily interested and unself-conscious.

Perhaps a few lines describing Cushla's physical appearance will help to complete the picture. She is a tall child, thin, but with well-rounded features, and attractively-set blue eyes. She has light golden-brown hair, and olive skin. She is still subject to skin rashes; her face quickly becomes blotchy when even mildly ill. She still shows the younger child's tendency to dribble occasionally, although this has decreased somewhat recently. Cushla's characteristic stance is with legs slightly apart and braced, arms held backward and turned outwards, and face turned slightly upwards in order to focus. If attending closely, or trying to take in a new situation, she often wears an expression of intensity. This is often accompanied by a degree of head movement, the whole attitude making her look different from other children. However, experience has shown that her 'strangeness' is produced by her efforts to compensate for handicapping features, and is actually sparked off by her determined intention to extract meaning from a scene, or situation. Time and, if necessary, training, is expected to decrease if not extinguish these characteristics.

When Cushla is focusing correctly, and particularly when she smiles or laughs, she is as any normal near-four-year-old – consumed by the joy of life and her own participation in it.

Other children usually like Cushla's frank and friendly approach. Not surprisingly, her home, with its abundance of books, toys, animals and play equipment, is a popular haunt for other children. It is noticeable that Cushla's parents are loved by many of her small friends, who increasingly stay the night at Karekare with the family. One can only assume that the endless patience, acceptance and love that have been characteristic of their care for Cushla have engendered in them qualities which other children intuitively recognise.

Chapter Seven

CUSHLA'S DEVELOPMENT IN THE LIGHT OF CURRENT DEVELOPMENTAL THEORY

Several critical, though perhaps unanswerable, questions present themselves when one considers Cushla's development from birth.

To what extent, for example, would one expect an otherwise normal child to be hampered by the handicaps that beset Cushla in her first year? It took Cushla seventeen months to achieve the fine-motor co-ordination of a six-months-old baby (see Gesell and Denver tests results, Chapter Three). For the duration of her first year of life, she was unable to pick up any object or hold it for more than a few seconds if it were placed in her hand. This disability barred her from using her mouth, in the characteristic way of babies, for feeling things. Nor could she sit up, or move about, and so explore her surroundings.

Again, Cushla's difficulty in focusing (which, current testing reveals, stems not from actual eye defect, but co-ordinatory difficulties between the eye and the brain) prevented her from experiencing her environment in a direct way. Compensatory help, which consisted of holding her very close to a person or object, and trying to ensure that she had achieved focus, was necessarily inferior to natural vision.

The effect of these handicaps on a healthy child might be expected to be considerable, and Cushla was not a healthy child. Ten weeks of her first fifty-two were spent in hospital, and, until she was ten months of age, a convulsive jerking reaction beset her at irregular intervals (often several times in a minute). Her breathing was rasping and shallow, and she was under almost constant treatment with antibiotics for chronic ear and throat infection.

A second question involves the extent to which, at birth, Cushla might have been described as 'otherwise normal'. There was clear indication that doctors, and others who dealt with her professionally, suspected that she was defective intellectually. Ordinary parents might have been forgiven for accepting this as a credible diagnosis, with consequent reduction of the measures they were prepared to apply to counteract the baby's handicaps.

It was Cushla's good fortune that her parents, while accepting her almost certain mental handicap, nonetheless embarked upon a course of sustained stimulation from which they have never wavered. Clearly, their acceptance and determination is receiving its reward in the production of an intelligent and happy child.

The third area of enquiry concerns, first, the extent to which the compensatory programme, if it may be classed as such, has ameliorated the effects of Cushla's handicaps, and, secondly, the extent to which involvement with picture books has helped her cognitive development. These are questions to which there is no sure answer, although it is hoped that the foregoing account casts some light, and reveals an occasional clue. In addition, it may be profitable to try to see Cushla's progress in the context of current theory of early human development. This, the following section attempts.

According to Piaget, the child from birth elaborates a more and more adequate knowledge of reality by acting on the external world. Inhelder (1962) says, using Piaget's theory to describe the process:

> It is precisely the successive forms of his (the child's) activity in the course of his development that determines his modes of knowledge.

What constituted 'the successive forms' of Cushla's activity?

At the sensory-motor stage, which he defines as from birth to two years, Piaget claims that there is no distinction between perceiving a thing and acting in response to it; at this stage, thought is, literally, action. Johanna Turner (1975) concludes from this:

> The infant thus develops by initially acting towards the immediately perceived environment, and subsequently by beginning to

87

internalise these actions so that he can, for example, think about his coming meal, although no meal is present.

Piaget (1974) gives in detail the following separate stages through which the child passes in his first year of life. In each case, an attempt is made to assess Cushla's degree of participation in the particular stage, bearing in mind her known handicaps.

In the first stage (birth to one month) complex reflexes, like those of sucking, give rise to a kind of exercise, which 'announces the formation of schemes in behaviour'. One can only assume that Cushla was able to participate at this level.

As early as the second stage (from one to four-and-a-half months) such schemes permit new acquisitions, for example, sucking of the thumb following fortuitous discovery. Cushla was, of course, prohibited from most forms of 'physical' discovery by the uselessness of her arms. However, most of her time at this stage was spent being held, or helped to 'play' by adults. At the same time, she was constantly helped to 'feel' objects with her mouth, but she could not learn to bring things to her mouth with her own hands. As described in Chapter One, she could move a hand towards a toy hung on the side of her cot if she was placed in the cot in such a way that her arms were fixed in front of her. There can be no way of knowing to what extent compensation was provided effectively, or indeed, the extent to which this provision was possible; the 'action' must be taken by the child in response to the immediately perceived environment, thereafter being internalised as a 'scheme', to use Piaget's term, if development is to take place.

Piaget's third stage occurs at about four-and-a-half months, and lasts until eight or nine months. During this period, the co-ordination of vision and prehension takes place; that is, the child can begin to grasp the object he sees intentionally. However, he has no idea of permanence; he does not know how to look under a cover to find a toy. This period, for Cushla, coincided with her confinement to a hospital cot. For most of the time, she was too ill for the application of compensatory measures, even if this were possible, and, presumably, cannot have made even minimal progress.

Certainly, her condition upon discharge indicated that she had actually regressed.

During the fourth stage of Piaget's progression (approximately the last quarter of the first year) the normal child

> . . . no longer limits himself to reproducing the sequences discovered by chance (circular reactions) but he uses the schemes thus discovered by co-ordinating them, one of these schemes assigning a goal to the action and one of the others serving as a means of achieving the goal. Or again, by presenting a new object, the child applies to it in turn (as exploration) each of the known schemes, in order to determine the practical significance or the use of this object, and he will grasp it to look at it, to suck it, etc; he will shake it, rub it against the side of the cradle, hit it with one hand while holding it with the other, etc. In short, the stage is characterised both by a growing mobility of the schemes of action and by the appearance of . . . the external co-ordination between acts of proxis.

At the specified age, Cushla could not perform any of the physical acts common to the normal baby.

She was described at thirty-five weeks as having 'no grasping ability'; the remark 'no development' constituted her adaptive 'score' on the Gesell Developmental Schedule (Chapter Two, p. 22).

Does this mean, in effect, that Cushla, not having been able in earlier stages to discover sequences by chance (circular reactions) and thereafter reproduce them intentionally, had not actually internalised appropriate 'schemes' and could therefore not be expected to be progressing cognitively? She could certainly not behave towards an object as Piaget suggests a baby who is "applying known schemes in order to determine the practical significance or the use of this object" does. What is needed here is evidence for the proposition that Cushla had actually built up a body of 'known schemes' although her physical handicaps prevented her from applying them in a practical way; and, by twelve months, that evidence was discernible.

To begin with, her vocalisation at twelve months was normal; at thirty-five weeks, on the Gesell scale, it was established at the thirty-two-week level, only three weeks behind her actual age, despite a lengthy period in hospital immediately prior to testing. By twelve months, she was actually identifying pictures of several objects in her books and had a recognisable spoken vocabulary of several words. Piaget says ". . . speech is bound up with thought and thus supposes a system of interiorised actions . . ." The conclusion that Cushla had developed 'a system of interiorised actions' is unavoidable.

Again, Piaget makes it clear that there are very different rhythms in individual growth; while the stages occur in a constant order of succession, "there are variations in the rapidity and duration of the development". It would seem to be of prime importance that a child's development be continuous, rather than that he fit neatly into a particular stage at a fixed age.

We are here, of course, concerned only with the very early stages of development. Elaborating further stages, Piaget reports the testing of schoolchildren in Martinique, who demonstrated "a four year lag in the acquisition of the notions of conservation deduction, seriation . . .", relating this to "an adult milieu lacking a dynamic intellectual quality . . ." and in general found that comparative studies made in different countries revealed "surprising delays". Discounting (as Piaget does) the intervention in these results of biological factors of maturation, we are left with the proposition that social factors – the effects of the particular environment to which the child is exposed – exercise some effect on the rate at which he will pass through all the essential stages, from birth onwards.

Given that Cushla's background provided, for her, a milieu of 'dynamic intellectual quality' (to invoke the term Piaget uses to describe the Martinique children's lack) is it not possible that her cognitive development was proceeding, if not at an average, normal rate, at least steadily in the first year of her life?

Bruner (1966) gives considerable support to the view that particular environments exercise a stimulating or debilitating effect on the developing child. "One finds no internal push to growth without a corresponding external pull" he says, and further, after defining the stages as he sees them (enactive, iconic and symbolic), suggests that, although instruction should be related to the mode of representation used by the child, growth should be encouraged by using the other modes wherever appropriate. In fact, Bruner contends that the skills involved in manipulating and handling the environment, in perceiving and imagining, and in symbolically representing it, can be taught in some form to children of any age.

It is not unlikely that Cushla's physical inability to participate in the stage at which, for both Piaget and Bruner, thought and action are inseparable, forced her parents to precipitate her into the next, or at any rate to expose her to it, at an unusually early age.

Cushla's physical disabilities may actually have acted as a facilitating factor here. Bruner describes the young child's perceptual attention as "highly unstable" and suggests that this may in part explain "the short supply of research on early perception". Cushla's perceptual attention was anything but 'unstable'; at nine months she would, after focusing on a picture presented to her in one of her books, look at it in a sustained and intent manner for several minutes, and at exactly eleven months, she recognised that a known picture was inverted, and tried to compensate (see Chapter Three pp. 33–34, 40–41).

Bruner describing the perceptual features of the iconic stage, which he envisages as beginning early in the second year, points out that the young child is an easy "victim of camouflage" and quotes the work of Witkin and colleagues (1962) in support of this. "By the same token", says Bruner "the young child (for example the three-year-old) seems ill-equipped to construct a picture from its parts, or complete it from partial clues", leading on to the conclusion that "there seems to be a considerable amount of 'one trackness' or need for serial integrity in the way figures are viewed – the child is easily thrown off by intersecting lines, by camouflage or by shared boundaries".

This would seem to indicate that the care taken to provide pictures with clear, uncluttered outlines (see Chapters Two and Three) was justified; and it might also in part, explain Cushla's attraction to black symbols on a plain page.

Vygotsky (1962) believes that thought and language begin as separate and independent activities; he instances the young child's attempts to reach objects, as evidence of thought without speech. The development of cognition and language, he suggests, is parallel yet interacting, until, at about two years of age, the curves meet, and "thought becomes verbal, and speech rational". It is possible to fit Cushla quite neatly into this scheme, but, once again, the fact that no real assessment of her handicap (in terms of the way Cushla herself experienced it) is possible, means that one can only speculate as to her mode of compensation at the 'action' level, if this existed.

Piaget says:

> During this first year, every later substructure is precisely constructed: the notion of object, that of space, that of time, in the form of temporal sequences, the notion of causality, in short the important notions later to be used by thought, and which are developed and used by material action as early as the sensory-motor level.

He adds that eighteen months of life is "quite inadequate" for the foundation of the substructures that must be laid down before the period of pre-operatory representation can begin, and suggests that development in the first year is "singularly accelerated".

There is reason to believe that Cushla's cognitive development, as she emerged from her first eighteen months of life, was not as far behind that of the average child as was at the time assumed, particularly by medical authorities; her unco-ordinated arm and eye behaviour at this stage lent her an appearance which, the evidence suggests, belied her actual level of cognitive attainment.

Cushla's subsequent speech development has been, as nearly as can be seen, normal, differing from the average child's only in the high proportion of references to her 'reading' that it contains.

Vygotsky and Piaget both describe the phenomenon of 'egocentric speech', in which the child talks aloud about his internal plans and actions, making no distinction between this speech for himself, and social speech for others. Here is Cushla, at three years, six months, talking to herself while drawing:

'That's like a monkey with a very fine tail, that's like a fish in a pond, that's like a fish in the sea . . . Look, here's a boat goes up again and down again. I draw a little teeny wee boat, I draw a big boat size. Look, I draw Topsy and Tim's name. I draw a little mousie playing with Agapanthus . . . that's a bit of finger . . . here's a little bed to sleep in, and here's a pillow . . .'

This might be any three or four-year-old thinking aloud; it is in the field of rote learning that Cushla's accomplishment is unusual. In volume, it has been prodigious, and unplanned; her parents had no way of knowing that this would be Cushla's reaction to their 'reading' programme. Is it possible to draw any conclusions concerning the possible effect of this learning of text by heart on Cushla's own generation of language?

Often, a phrase or sentence 'takes over' when Cushla starts to talk, e.g. (3.5), "there's a cat . . . to sit on the doorstep or purr by the fire" (from *The Little Wooden Farmer*), almost as if the words slip out unbidden. Recently, she has given some sign of realising this herself, e.g. (3.8), 'Now I'm going shopping. Hey, Mum, forgot the cheque book! Forgot that cats can't fly, but most of all, forgot the cat flap!' (*Mog, the Forgetful Cat*). Laughed: 'I'm silly, eh?' Her manner on this occasion indicated that she was referring to her interpolation, not her forgetfulness.

Cushla's vocabulary certainly reflects this conversance with books. Words and phrases of increasing complexity and expressiveness are used correctly: 'doing nothing in particular', 'an amazing sight', 'terribly frightened', 'difficult', 'silent', 'strange', 'ridiculous'. At the time of writing, she gets in first while listening to *Make Way for Ducklings* by Robert McCloskey, with "a great responsibility", and "bursting with pride", phrases which are used to describe the duck parents' attitude to the new ducklings. Cushla's expression, a model of expansive satisfaction, leaves no doubt that these phrases, unheard several weeks ago, have acquired meaning and will be available for use before long in other contexts.

As mentioned earlier (Chapter Five, p. 70), Carroll in 1939 suggested that the learning of rote material as an important factor in speech development merited investigation. It is difficult to avoid the conclusion that, if a particular child has demonstrated her ability to 'take' from the material read aloud and committed to memory words and phrases which she has then used appropriately in other contexts, she has thereby added to her speech repertoire, and, therefore, her cognitive equipment. It certainly seems that Cushla has done this, and is continuing to do it: in her case at any rate, the learning of rote material has made its contribution to her speech development.

Joan Tough, author of *Focus on Meaning* (1973), a book sub-titled 'Talking to some purpose with young children', and designed to 'help the teacher, the parent and all concerned with growing children to gain insight into the part that language plays during the early years of childhood', defines the home environment which provides optimum opportunity for the development of language which will simultaneously express and promote the child's thinking. She describes the background of a three-year-old boy, in particular his relationship to the adults in his family. The adult, for Mark, is one who "offers information, who invites thought and discussion . . . He learns that to ask questions brings information, to try to solve problems brings approval, and that language makes past experience live again." The child reflects this relationship, and the example of parents who themselves use complex speech forms to discuss, anticipate, plan and consider, in his own speech; he is acquiring the 'tools of thinking'.

James Britton (1971) says, "the habit of verbalising originates in, and is fostered above all by speech with an adult", and Luria and Yudovich (1959) in their work with the identical twins Liosha and Yura showed beyond any doubt that "retarded speech and backward behaviour" in certain cases are intertwined, both, in this case, responding to a programme of intervention which consisted in great part of "speech with an adult".

This, Cushla had, from her very earliest days. Even when it seemed that she could understand not at all, she was talked to constantly. Every effort has been made to answer her questions, and to keep her thinking. The following recording was made when Cushla was exactly three years, six months old.

C. 'Mummy, did you see the horse before?'
M. 'No. Where was it?'

C. 'Um, it was, . . . it was . . . um, I can't think properly at the moment.'

M. 'Was it on your bed?' (Suggesting toy horse – M. thought it was probably the horse in the paddock next door, but wanted Cushla to provide information.)

C. 'No.'

M. 'Was it on the top you were playing with?' (Picture.)

C. 'No! I told you I can't think at the moment. Everybody can't think at the moment sometimes. You say, "I can't think at the moment," Mum. I heard you last morning.'

M. 'Yes, I know, often I can't remember where things are.'

C. (Shouting.) 'No! Not remember! Just can't think!'

It seems highly unlikely that Cushla understands the difference between 'can't think properly' and 'can't remember'; experience shows that she takes up a new expression and uses it wherever possible, and for several days after this extract, she could not 'think properly' on numerous occasions. But the conclusion that she was playing with ideas is unavoidable. ('Last morning' continues in use; presumably derived from 'last night'.) This extract, and many others, illustrates the way in which Cushla has been listened to, encouraged to express her meaning by supplying supporting detail, and, above all, the way in which, for Cushla, it is now possible to use words "not *with* objects but *in place* of them" to use Britton's phrase.

No mention has been made so far of Cushla's possible biological inheritance. The inference is present that, as every one of her cells carries an abnormality, this must obviously include the brain cells. The effects of this abnormality are probably unknowable; only Cushla's achievement can give any clue, and then only in a general way. Certainly, both of her parents are of above average intelligence and education, but again, although speculation as to what basic intelligence Cushla might have inherited is possible, no conclusion can be reached. Such speculation, therefore seems profitless. The only certainty is that her parents' intelligence, and their determined application of that intelligence to her problems have played a major part in Cushla's achievements.

95

Conclusion

Cushla's story has several separate but interweaving threads.

It can be seen as an account of physical development against a background of constant illness and occasional crisis. At the same time, it is possible to trace the emergence of an active intelligence from a mind originally ill-served by its instruments of sight and touch; a mind which may well have been defective to begin with.

But if her story is to have implication for other children, its special features must be identified and illuminated. And these exist.

It is not enough to say that Cushla's parents were intelligent and vigorous, courageous and accepting, for these are qualities that describe many of the parents who face the prospect of bringing up a handicapped child. Nor is it true to suggest that they merely worked harder than other parents might at implementing known ways of treating a multi-handicapped baby.

Cushla's history is different because of the nature of the intervention that occurred; and the nature of the intervention arose from factors in her background which have been described in foregoing chapters.

These factors do not need to be elaborated further. It is enough to say that Cushla's parents shared a deep and intuitive conviction that the experience of close, consistent contact with those who loved her, and were prepared to 'be her eyes and her hands' against the day when she might find her own, constituted her strongest hope for the future.

Several fortunate circumstances certainly existed. There was the contact which made it possible for the family to approach the Education Department of the University of Auckland, leading to subsequent testing and continued interest. Again, through a family

96

business, the parents had access to a supply of picture books and help with the selection of suitable titles (though the parents quickly learned, through trial and error, the features which marked a book out as suitable for Cushla's needs).

These factors, and the help that her parents were able to call on, played their part. Cushla's needs were sensed rather than recognised; response, however slight, to a particular procedure, was accepted as an indication that a particular line might be profitable to pursue. Experimentation was constant.

Yet another thread runs through Cushla's story; the assumption on the part of all newly-consulted doctors that the baby was mentally retarded. Not all have been as abrupt as the G.P. who, on seeing Cushla for the first time at eighteen months, told her mother that she was 'not normal', urged her to accept this fact, and offered to make arrangements for her to be cared for on a daily basis at the Intellectually Handicapped Children's Centre in a neighbouring suburb; but the baby's parents came to accept the fact that superficial observation of Cushla's behaviour usually induced this view, and that doctors were no more likely than anyone else to look beyond the unco-ordinated eyes and overall inability to meet accepted physical standards.

Apprehension is surely justified when one considers the near-reverence with which many people accept statements from the medical profession. How many young mothers would have accepted this 'diagnosis' and the accompanying well-meant offer: Cushla's abnormality had been accepted by her family since very early in her life. At eighteen months they had reason to believe that she was making good progress and that this progress was, at least in part, the result of their encouragement and stimulation. The label 'not normal' seemed to them irrelevant, the advice a mockery of their efforts. Cushla's mother is an exceptionally strong and realistic young woman, but she came nearer to despair at that moment than at any other time in the baby's life.

Again, when Cushla was just over two, her mother was obliged to listen while 'mental retardation' was diagnosed by successive doctors, this time paediatricians in training. Permission had been requested by the hospital, and willingly given, for Cushla to be 'used' in an examination. (Apparently, she had the doubtful distinction of exhibiting more unrelated defects than any other child available!)

Cushla's mother was in no way disturbed by this suggestion; she had become used to hearing it voiced, and the doctors concerned were obviously intent upon identifying as many defects as possible. But again, one wonders if any other child has ever been labelled 'retarded' simply because his eyes did not focus, his hands and arms hung limp, and he was inclined to dribble? One is impelled to question the necessity for labels, containing as they do the implication that rigid boundaries divide 'normal' and 'abnormal' human beings – as if the very quality of humanity varies, as 'borderlines' are crossed.

And one wonders also at the dearth of help and advice for the parents of a baby with handicaps. Surely, effort and organisation, rather than finance, could go some distance to providing this? As a start, could not medical authorities themselves affirm the need for stimulation and constant close attention for the baby who will find learning hard? As in many other situations, damage can be done by parents who sincerely wish to do the best possible but, without instruction, have no way of identifying 'the best'.

A note of hope should be inserted here. When Cushla's small sister was six weeks old, the family was asked (by the Psychiatric Department of the hospital) to co-operate in demonstrating to medical students that a family containing a handicapped child can be happy and normal. Accordingly, parents and both children appeared in a 'one-way' viewing situation with unseen audience. Both adults confessed to feeling rather uncomfortable at this rather contrived performance, but soon relaxed as Cushla played cheerfully with toys and puzzles provided, brought books to be read and generally interacted with the others in her family. It must have been apparent to the students that Cushla, although she had obvious handicaps, still had much in common with the average child. The session concluded with an interview during which Cushla's mother (the rest of the family having withdrawn) answered a psychiatrist's questions about Cushla's history and her own and her husband's reaction to their parenthood.

It is gratifying to realise that doctors in training are being encouraged to regard families as social units, and to consider the effects of handicapped children on the family situation. Unfortunately, there is little evidence that many doctors already in practice demonstrate a depth of understanding and knowledge about the needs of either the child or his family. There are certainly exceptions to this rule; but there is no guarantee that the average parents facing the anguish and exhaustion of caring for a child with handicaps will have help, advice and, above all, understanding, in the years that lie ahead.

Cushla's parents acknowledge in full the support and understanding they have received from the paediatrician at the Auckland Hospital, to whose care the baby was assigned after her first period in hospital at nine months. This young woman has never been concerned with classification or labelling. To her, as to the parents, 'Cushla is Cushla', a child who may have difficulty in developing her full potential, and therefore merits help.

However, although many children with mental handicaps also have physical handicaps, many others do not, and may have no contact in the very early years with any outside agency.

Barney (1975) quotes the Younghusband Report (the outcome of a working party on children with special needs set up by the National Bureau for Co-operation in Child Care in London, in 1970) as saying:

> What is now known about the importance of early learning applies with even greater force to the young handicapped child. Thus, it is of vital importance to evoke pre-school facilities, be it nursery schools, playgrounds, or home teaching, in some cases even before the age of two years.

Cushla's 'home-teaching' programme was under way from the time it was first realised that she seemed 'cut off' from others – that is, almost from birth. For how many other babies is this condition, whatever its cause, unrecognised and untreated? How much improvement would society ultimately see in its supposedly 'retarded' children if compensatory intervention always occurred at this early stage and continued in the atmosphere of concern and support that Cushla has always had, as of right?

Cushla's parents also pay tribute to the Crippled Children's Society, from which they now receive considerable help: swimming lessons and use of special play equipment for Cushla, and the opportunity of meeting other families with similar problems. The Parents' Centre movement, the early playgroup, and now Play Centre have all in their way also contributed to the family's well-being and helped Cushla towards the realisation of her full capacity.

One is, however, constantly aware that the crucial stage in Cushla's life was the very earliest period, the stage at which she might have relapsed into a world of dimly-perceived impression, progressively falling behind both physically and intellectually. How can one estimate the degree of handicap that she might now exhibit if this had been allowed to happen? And what about the children for whom no such in-built programme exists?

David Barney, speaking of the need for specific 'teaching' sessions for the handicapped child, says:

There is no reason why such contrived learning sessions should not be enjoyable fun experiences – possibly more so than random, poorly motivated play.

Cushla's development provides living proof of the effectiveness of "learning sessions." Her confidence and her cheerfulness attest absolutely to the absence of that 'sense of worthlessness, dependency and depression' which, Barney further suggests, may arise from the neglect of the child's need for special instruction.

That such sessions can be "enjoyable fun experiences" is unquestionable, when the alternatives available to the handicapped child are considered.

Cushla's future is uncertain, and major decisions lie ahead. What sort of school should she attend, and should entry be delayed?

There is evidence that she will need, for some time to come, a one-to-one teaching situation if her progress is to be maintained. To quote David Barney again:

Current thinking, as revealed in the literature, appears to be increasingly recommending structured programmes, individually prescribed, for the young handicapped. Opportunities for voluntary or incidental learning, as found in the traditional type pre-school programme, appear to be inadequate and less appropriate for these children.

This is certainly true for Cushla at the moment and may continue so for some time. Play Centre provides the stimulation of other children; home, with its constant emphasis on the one-to-one teaching and learning situation, equips Cushla for regular sorties into the group. One might even speculate that the success of her contact with the group depends on the continuing success of the individual teaching programme. Cushla is coping, increasingly, with a group situation, recognising her own special friends, and joining in imaginative play with other children. But she is often confused by the speed of impression. She needs to be shown, and to be told, individually. It seems likely that she might be suited by part-time school attendance, reinforced by continuing home instruction, which, her parents have demonstrated, they are well able to provide.

Specific training, combined with appropriate physiotherapy, is expected to reduce or eliminate some of Cushla's 'differences' – her unusual arm attitude, her rather shambling gait, and her tendency to dribble. She is currently undergoing dental treatment at the Auckland Hospital. Constant ill-health, combined with the effect of necessary drugs, has led, not surprisingly, to considerable dental decay. As usual, one of her parents is always with Cushla, and, as usual, she seems to understand or at least accept, the need for this treatment.

Now that the biggest physical hurdle, the correction of her kidney abnormality, has been passed, it is hoped that her progress will proceed steadily, and that more uninterrupted time will be available. For time has always been short for Cushla; time to practise skills which did not come easily, time to capitalise on what had been learned already, time to gather strength after the debilitations of constant infection and the endless round of hospital visits and tests. And not only have the periods of interruption been constant and lengthy; Cushla's sensory handicaps have made 'intake' a difficult, often tortuous business at the best of times.

Cushla's good fortune in her parents cannot be measured. Accepting her as 'a child with handicaps' they have avoided speculation and simply done what seemed to them to be appropriate and possible from day to day. One suspects that their measures might well have been less than possible for people of smaller spirit. Cushla herself must stand as proof of their appropriateness.

And how can one assess the contribution of her books to the quality of Cushla's life?

It seems clear that access to such a wealth of words and pictures, in a setting of consistent love and support, has contributed enormously to her cognitive development in general and her language in particular. It is hoped that the foregoing chapters have established this.

But perhaps, most of all, Cushla's books have surrounded her with friends; with people and warmth and colour during the days when her life was lived in almost constant pain and frustration. The adults who have loved her and have tried to represent the world to her when she could not do this for herself have played their parts. But perhaps it was the characters themselves who went with her into the dark and lonely places that only she knew.

And perhaps they will always be with her; Peter Rabbit and Grandmother Lucy, Mr Gumpy and James, James, followed by a procession of cats and kings, tigers and bears, with Davy and Emma and Naughty Agapanthus bringing up the rear. If so, she will be well fortified.

Perhaps Cushla's own words, recorded on 18 August 1975, when she was three years, eight months old, tell us all we need to know. They were spoken as she settled herself on the sofa, her rag doll in her arms and the usual pile of books at her side: 'Now I can read to Looby Lou, 'cause she's tired and sad, and she needs a cuddle and a bottle and a book.'

Surely a prescription for any child, with or without handicaps.

Postscript

Two-and-a-half years have passed since Cushla's story was first told. 'What is she like now?' hangs in the air, an obvious question.

At six-and-a-quarter, Cushla has much in common with the average child of like age. She is energetic, loving, demanding and generous; alternately protective towards, and exasperated by, her small sister; usually co-operative but sometimes stubborn . . . a child of spirit, humour and warmth, sure of her place in the world, and determined to have her share of its joy. She has had, already, more than her share of its pain.

There has been a major change in Cushla's life during this period. Her father now has his own pottery workshop in the house, and his own kiln outside. Stephen cares for both little girls while their mother goes to work each day. Patricia works as statistics co-ordinator for a large company in Auckland, and is this year completing a post-graduate diploma at the university, at her firm's instigation. This rearrangement of family roles has brought many advantages: an opportunity for Stephen to develop a creative flair for which spare time was never available before, and the chance for Patricia to enjoy fresh experiences and to use a qualification all but forgotten during the intense and worrying years of Cushla's babyhood.

Perhaps, most of all, it has given a new flavour to the little girls' lives. Always deeply involved with his children, Stephen is now able to include them in his life and interests in a unique way. His pottery is starting to be known and bought in Auckland. The venture has passed from a tentative beginning to a period of steady and satisfying growth.

Cushla and her books

The reversal of parent roles was smoothly accomplished in this family. 'Steve' and 'Trisha' as the little girls commonly call them have always shared work rather than allocating functions. They share, too, a conviction that people matter more than things, and that available money should be used to support and extend interests rather than to increase possessions. Predictably, their comfortable, shabby old house is full of books and the evidence of family hobbies. The furniture is old or improvised and the walls adorned with home-made wall hangings, posters and the children's paintings. A large sprung mattress, on the floor in the living room, is an ideal roosting place for children, pets and parents. Here books are read and games played. A sagging, comfortable old couch in the corner of the pottery workshop houses the little girls, their books and their toys when Stephen's work demands an uninterrupted spell at wheel or bench and he must ensure their safety at the same time. A wide set of french windows, bought secondhand and installed in one wall of the workshop, gives on to a sheltered terrace at the back of the house, where the children play within sight and hearing. In front, a tall home-built brushwood fence encloses the property. On the bank behind, in summer, old, crimson-flowered pohutukawa trees lean towards the house. Inside, in winter, the smell of wood burning in the open fire mingles with the tang of herbs and spices from the big, shelved pantry which Stephen has built. Always, night and day, beyond the steep cliff which separates the end of the narrow valley from the deep, rock-walled beach, breakers from the wild Tasman crash on to the shore. But the earliest settler chose his spot well, and the house is snug.

The extent and nature of Cushla's difficulties have become clearer as she has shrugged off the trappings of babyhood and turned into a school-age child. Inadequate hearing has been added to her list of handicaps, and hopes that she would overcome her manual difficulties at an early age have proven over-optimistic. But her inability to write merely illuminates her capacity for reading, and Cushla continues to try. This, after all, has always been her response to the apparently impossible. Time has shown it to be a profitable one.

Cushla's fascination with the printed word has never flagged. She now reads fluently – preferably silently, unless she is reading to Sanchia (there needs to be some *point* in reading aloud). She is currently enthusiastic about public signs and notices, treasure hunts which involve complicated written instructions, and receiving letters from obliging relations.

Phrases from books are still heard, but are often hard to identify now that she reads silently. 'Feathers and Foxgloves!' as an expletive baffled everyone until it turned up in *Tom Fox and the Apple Pie*, by Clyde Watson at next borrowing from the library. 'Good lack-a-day!' fell into constant use after Hoffmann's *Tom Thumb* was read aloud to both little girls.

Cushla was not 'taught' to read, unless the provision of language and story, in books and out of books, can be called a method.

I believe it can, and that it is the best method of all. It produces children who experience reading as a joyous process, natural to the human state; children who absorb ideas as sponges absorb water. That this eager ingestion helps such children to find meaning in the complex and contradictory experiences that constitute life is self-evident.

Cushla's voice is still thin and rather husky, her verbal response often delayed. It takes time for her to organise her breathing and sound production, and one senses that the thoroughness of her thought further complicates the process. She has a habit of keeping up a running commentary to herself on whatever is happening. On occasion, she reveals considerable insight.

'Everyone is surprised that I have learned to skip. They didn't think I'd be able to skip when I came today. Grandpa is saying "Good heavens! Cushla has learned to skip!" '

This was a comment on family reaction to a demonstrated new skill: skipping. It had been achieved with Cushla's well-known application; the performance had required rigid concentration. The family, Grandpa included, had expressed only congratulation. No one had confessed to surprise, however reasonable.

Cushla has been in hospital four times during the past two years. A nose operation to improve her breathing and an ear operation to prevent further hearing loss have both been performed. One of her frequent falls resulted in a skull fracture, which fortunately healed without complication. (A specially constructed crash helmet prescribed and made by the hospital continues to attract the envy and admiration of small friends.)

Karekare Valley now has a school. The Lone Kauri Community School which opened in February 1978 is a unique institution, even for rural New Zealand. It is conducted in a barn in a bush clearing, and has six pupils. The children, all aged either five or six, are enrolled in the Government Correspondence School. But the young man who watches over them is much more than a supervisor. It is the community's good fortune that their number includes a qualified teacher who knows the children and their parents intimately, and who finds this unconventional setting (his own barn) an ideal place in which to tend his small but active flock while their real schoolhouse is built by voluntary local labour.

The novelty of their situation has already caught the public's fancy, and articles have appeared in national and local newspapers. Both have featured pictures of six healthy, casually-clad children of the same size, deeply involved in a school life which they find natural and satisfying. One of them is Cushla. Her teacher knows that she is special . . . but then, to him, so are the four boys and the other girl . . .

Sanchia, now approaching four, is a serene child. Her Spanish name means 'saintly' and she has, indeed, a madonna-like beauty. Reassuringly, she reacts with spirit to any infringement of her rights. But she is a loving, biddable child, intelligent and mature. No one has concerned themselves with providing Sanchia with books suited to her age. Just beyond babyhood, she showed a preference for books that suited Cushla, two-and-a-half years her senior. This has continued.

Recently, I read them both the Heins-Hyman edition of *Snow White*. At the end, when the wicked queen is obliged to dance in red-hot iron slippers until she falls down dead, I faltered. Then, remembering that they owned and loved the Jarrell-Burkert version, which also adheres to this original form, I took heart and went on. There was a short silence, as the story ended. Then Sanchia said in her surprisingly low-pitched, rather earthy, New Zealand voice, 'Yeah. Serve her right'. No nonsense about this little girl.

And none about Cushla either. Before all else, she is a realistic child. She knows that life is hard, and painful, and that sometimes only despair seems to be justified. But she knows also that life is wonderful and rewarding, and that as we have to live it anyway we had best get on with it. Cushla Yeoman, my granddaughter, a child of hardy and humorous spirit, is getting on with it very well indeed at the moment.

Seven years ago, before Cushla was born, I would have laid claim to a deep faith in the power of books to enrich children's lives. By comparison with my present conviction, this faith was a shallow thing. I know now what print and picture have to offer a child who is cut off from the world, for whatever reason. But I know also that there must be another human being, prepared to intercede, before anything can happen. Had she been born to other parents – however intelligent and well-intentioned – Cushla might never have encountered, as a baby, word and picture between the covers of a book. Certainly, no authority prescribes reading aloud for chronically ill babies whose handicaps are thought to be mental as well as physical.

It is in the hope of recruiting more human links between books and the handicapped children of the world that Cushla's parents have agreed to the publication of her story. We are all confident that a much older Cushla will want to help with this recruitment. We think that Cushla's belief in books as bridges may be even stronger than ours.

Appendix A

Chart showing Cushla's interaction with books and stories on a typical day, 3 March, 1975.

TIME	TITLE		C'S BEHAVIOUR AND REACTIONS ★ Suggested + Read by
7.30 am.			Playing with weights of scales. 'This teeny-weeny one, this middle-sized one, this great-big one.' Correct.
8.30 am.	Joan Baez Song Book (adult)	★C +C	Flipped over pages, sang 'Here we go Looby Lou', 'Baa baa Black Sheep' and 'Twinkle, Twinkle Little Star'. Has seen father singing from this book but not for over three weeks.
9.00 am.	Puppies and Kittens	★C	Picked out dogs like Nellie and Carla, and cat like Mime. Likes this book currently – seems to enjoy likening animals to 'real' pets.
9.30 am.			Putting doll to sleep, 'Sleep baby sleep, father guards sheep' (from *Hush-a-Bye Rhymes*). Knows whole verse.

TIME	TITLE	C'S BEHAVIOUR AND REACTIONS ★ Suggested + Read by	
10.15 am			Playing with three loaves of bread (different sizes) 'This teeny-weeny loaf bread' etc. Correct again.
10.30 am.	Animals' Lullaby (twice)	★ M + M	Read twice, to settle C. (crying) Successful. Always very involved with this book. As usual, asked 'Why?' constantly throughout.
11.05 am.	Scuffy the Tugboat	★ C + M	Not very interested in this book, although suggested it. But loves introduction: 'Scuffy is a small red tugboat with a bright blue smokestack.' As usual, repeated this with relish.
11.15 am.			'Me got my beautiful little red coat . . .' Appeared from bedroom flourishing her new red cardigan. (*Little Black Sambo*).
11.30 am.	The Christmas Book (twice)	★ M + M	C's books recently arranged in bookcase with spines showing. M. suggested story, C. chose this one by recognising spine (yellow, book turquoise) saying, 'Read book about angels'.
11.40 am.	Mr Gumpy's Outing	★ C + M	Only comment: 'Me don't like Mr Gumpy today'. Usually a favourite.

Cushla and her books

TIME	TITLE	C'S BEHAVIOUR AND REACTIONS ★ Suggested + Read by	
12.30 pm.	Wildsmith Mother Goose	★C +C	This book was packed away with our 'good' books when we moved, and was unpacked only few days ago. First time C. allowed to read it alone. Extremely careful. Read it for 20 mins, continually commenting on pictures, e.g. 'This lady tired in bed', 'This man got funny hat on'.
12.55 pm.	When We Were Very Young	★M +M	Meant to put C. to sleep – unsuccessful. Tired, but interested. No comment.
1.20 pm.	Young Puffin Book of Verse (to p. 101)	★M +M	Did not read every poem – usually one or two from each opening. C. went to sleep on M's knee.
2.15 pm.	The Christmas Book	★C +M	Requested book forcefully on waking. Seems fascinated with the kings, star, angels, baby. Pointed things out and really took part in story. Said, 'Me got star like that in my bedroom' – showed M. light in bedroom.
3-5 pm.			At beach.
4.30 pm.			'Let's walk home across the fields, it's time for tea.' Said on beach when C. wanted to come home. (*Mr Gumpy's Outing*)

TIME	TITLE		C's BEHAVIOUR AND REACTIONS ★ Suggested + Read by
5.10 pm.	Old Dame Trot	★C +M	C. can finish any line in this book. Loves picking out the mouse on each page.
5.20 pm.	Animals' Lullaby	★C +C	Flipped through, gabbling the words, got the essence of each page. Then sang 'Hush Little Baby' at length, on last page.
5.45 pm.	Wildsmith Mother Goose	★C +M	'This great big huge strong book', handed it to M. Remembered 'Two little Dicky Birds' from yesterday and got fingers ready page before.
7.00 pm.			Talking to father: 'Harry played by the railway and got dirtier still'. (*Harry the Dirty Dog*).
8.00 pm.	Owl and the Pussycat (3 times)	★F +F	To put C. to sleep. Successful.

BOOKS IN CUSHLA'S LIBRARY
together with those used by Carol White at a similar age
(Listed are publishers of USA editions; USA paperback editions are also noted. Books not published in USA are listed with name of UK publisher.)

FOUR TO SEVEN MONTHS

Author	*Title*
Bruna, Dick	*A Story to Tell* Methuen 1975
Lear, Edward	*The Owl and the Pussycat* Mowbray 1970 (UK)
Oxenbury, Helen	*ABC of Things* Watts 1972
Potter, Beatrix	*Appley Dapply's Nursery Rhymes* Warne 1917
Wildsmith, Brian	*Mother Goose* Watts 1965; paper 1965

EIGHT TO NINE MONTHS

Bruna, Dick	*B is for Bear* Methuen 1977
Bruna, Dick	*I Can Count* Methuen 1975
Janus, Grete	*Teddy* Sadler 1968 (UK)
Mitgutsch, Ali	*Beside the Busy Sea* Collins 1972 (UK)
Mitgutsch, Ali	*In the Busy Town* Collins 1972 (UK)
Peppé, Rodney	*The House that Jack Built* Delacorte 1970
Petersham, Maude and Miska	*The Box with Red Wheels* Macmillan 1949; paper 1972
Ryder, Eileen	*Whose Baby is It?* Burke 1973 (UK)

NINE TO EIGHTEEN MONTHS

Author	*Title*
Adamson, Jean and Gareth	*Hop Like Me* Whitman 1972
Ainsworth, Ruth	*What Can I See?* Bancroft 1972 (UK)
Carle, Eric	*Do You Want to Be My Friend?* Crowell 1971
Clure, Beth and Rumsey, Helen	*Little, Big, Bigger* Bowmar 1968
Clure, Beth and Rumsey, Helen	*Where Is Home?* Bowmar 1968
Ivory, Lesley Anne	*At Home* Burke 1970 (UK)
Lenski, Lois	*Davy's Day* Walck 1943
Lenski, Lois	*Papa Small* Walck 1951
Martin, Bill	*Brown Bear, Brown Bear* Holt 1971
Ryder, Eileen	*Whose Baby Is It?* Burke 1973 (UK)
Ryder, Eileen	*Who Are We?* Burke 1972 (UK)
Ryder, Eileen	*What Do We Like?* Burke 1972 (UK)
Ryder, Eileen	*What Colour Is It?* Burke 1972 (UK)
Stowell, Gordon	*Smells I Like* Mowbray 1969 (UK)
Thomson, Ross	*A Noisy Book* Scroll 1973
Zacharias, Thomas and Wanda	*But Where Is the Green Parrot?* Delacorte/Seymour Lawrence 1968

EIGHTEEN MONTHS TO THREE YEARS

Adamson, Jean and Gareth	*Topsy and Tim's Birthday Party* Blackie 1971 (UK)
Ainsworth, Ruth	*Jill and Peter* Bancroft 1965 (UK)
Ainsworth, Ruth	*Susan's House* Bancroft 1966 (UK)
Alberti, Trude	*The Animals' Lullaby* Bodley Head 1967 (UK)
Aliki	*Hush Little Baby* Prentice 1968
Berg, Leila	*That Baby* Macmillan 1972 (UK)
Breinburg, Petronella	*Shawn Goes to School* Crowell 1974 (UK title *My Brother Sean*)
Bright, Robert	*The Friendly Bear* Doubleday 1957; paper 1971

Cushla and her books

Author	Title
Brown, Margaret Wise	*A Child's Goodnight Book* Addison-Wesley 1943
Bruna, Dick	*The King* Methuen 1975
Bruna, Dick	*Snuffy* Methuen 1975
Bruna, Dick	*The Sailor* Methuen 1966 (UK)
Burningham, John	*Mr Gumpy's Outing* Holt 1971
Carle, Eric	*The Very Hungry Caterpillar* Collins 1972
Emberley, Barbara and Ed	*Drummer Hoff* Prentice 1967
Ets, Marie Hall	*Play With Me* Viking 1955
Flack, Marjorie	*Ask Mr Bear* Macmillan 1932; paper 1971
Fons, Benny	*What's the Matter, Lucy?* Methuen 1973 (UK)
Gàg, Wanda	*The ABC Bunny* Coward 1933
Gagg, M. E.	*Helping at Home* Merry Thoughts (n.d.)
Gagg, M. E.	*Puppies and Kittens* Merry Thoughts (n.d.)
Galdone, Paul	*The Old Woman and her Pig* McGraw 1961
Heeronymis, De	*All the Day Long* Methuen 1972 (UK)
Hoskyns, K.	*Boots* Longman 1966 (UK)
Hutchins, Pat	*Titch* Macmillan 1971
Lear, Edward	*Nonsense Songs* Chatto 1953 (UK)
Lemke, Horst	*Places and Faces* Scroll 1971
Lenski, Lois	*Davy and His Dog* Walck 1957
Lenski, Lois	*The Little Farm* Walck 1942; paper (n.d.)
Lenski, Lois	*Let's Play House* Walck 1944
Low, Alice	*Summer* Random/Beginner 1963
Massie, Diane Redfield	*The Baby Beebee Bird* Harper 1978
Milne, A. A.	*When We Were Very Young* Dutton 1961; paper Dell 1975

Author	*Title*
Minarik, Else Holmelund	
ill. by Sendak, Maurice	*Little Bear* Harper 1957; paper 1978
Oxenbury, Helen	*The Great Big Enormous Turnip* Heinemann 1968 (UK)
Potter, Beatrix	*The Story of a Fierce Bad Rabbit* Warne 1906
Potter, Beatrix	*The Tale of Peter Rabbit* Warne 1902; paper Dover 1972
Potter, Beatrix	*The Tale of Tom Kitten* Warne 1907
Roffey, Maureen	*A Bookload of Animals* Bodley Head 1973 (UK)
Tudor, Tasha	*First Poems of Childhood* Platt 1967
Virin, Anna	*Elsa's Bears* Harvey 1978
Wood, Anne (ed)	*Hush-a-Bye Rhymes* Storychair 1972 (UK)
Wood, Joyce	
ill. by Francis, Frank	*Grandmother Lucy and her Hats* Atheneum 1969
Zion, Gene	*Harry the Dirty Dog* Harper 1956
ill. by Graham, Margaret B.	

THREE YEARS TO THREE YEARS THREE MONTHS

Ainsworth, Ruth	*At the Zoo* Bancroft 1965 (UK)
Bowes, Clare	*How Many?* Longman 1972 (UK)
Brown, Margaret Wise	
ill. by Weisgard, Leonard	*The Indoor Noisy Book* Harper 1942; paper 1976
Bruna, Dick	*The Christmas Book* Methuen 1964
Burningham, John	*Mr Gumpy's Motor Car* Crowell 1976; paper Penguin 1977
Carle, Eric	*Animals and Their Babies* Crowell 1975
Domanska, Janina	*The Little Red Hen* Macmillan 1973
Elkin, Benjamin	*Big Jump and Other Stories* Random/Beginner 1958

Cushla and her books

Author	Title
Françoise	*Springtime for Jeanne-Marie* Scribner 1955
Galdone, Paul	*The Three Bears* Seabury 1972
Galdone, Paul	*The Three Billy Goats Gruff* Seabury 1973
Ireson, Barbara (ed)	*The Young Puffin Book of Verse* paper Penguin 1976
Kerr, Judith	*Mog, The Forgetful Cat* Parents 1972
Kerr, Judith	*The Tiger Who Came to Tea* Coward 1968
Krasilovsky, Phyllis ill. by Ninon	*The Very Little Girl* Doubleday 1953; paper (n.d.)
Mayer, Mercer	*Me and My Flying Machine* Collins 1973 (UK)
Peterson, Hans	*"I Don't Want To," Said Sara* Burke 1968 (UK)
Wildsmith, Brian	*The Lazy Bear* Watts 1974
Wing, R.	What Is Big? (in *Sounds of Numbers*) Holt 1966
Wolde, Gunilla	*This Is Betsy* Random 1975 (UK title *Emma Quite Contrary*)

THREE YEARS THREE MONTHS TO THREE YEARS NINE MONTHS

Aliki	*Go Tell Aunt Rhody* Macmillan 1974
Beckman, Kaj	*Lisa Cannot Sleep* Watts 1970 (UK title *Susan Cannot Sleep*)
Berends, Polly B.	*Who's That in the Mirror?* Random 1965
Berenstain, Stan and Jan	*Bears in the Night* Random 1971
Brown, Myra B.	*First Night Away from Home* Heinemann 1961 (UK)
Charlip, Remy	*Fortunately* Parents 1964
Cunliffe, John	*Farmer Barnes and Bluebell* Lion 1970

Author	*Title*
Dalgliesh, Alice	*The Little Wooden Farmer*
ill. by Lobel, Anita	Macmillan 1968
Fisher, Aileen	*Going Places* Nelson 1973
ill. by Quenell, Midge	
Fletcher, Elizabeth	*The Little Goat*
	Storyteller 1971 (UK)
Freeman, Don	*Corduroy* Viking 1968;
	paper Penguin 1976
Gàg, Wanda	*Millions of Cats* Coward 1928;
	paper 1977
Galdone, Paul	*The Moving Adventures of Old*
	Dame Trot McGraw 1972
	(UK title *Old Dame Trot*)
Gergely, Tibor	*Scuffy the Tugboat* Golden 1972
Gordon, Giles and Margaret	*Walter and the Balloon*
	Heinemann 1974
Grimm, Bros.	*The Elves and the Shoemaker*
ill. by Brandt, Katrin	Bodley Head 1968 (UK)
Howell, Margaret	*The Lonely Dragon*
	Kestrel 1972 (UK)
Hutchins, Pat	*The Wind Blew* Macmillan 1974
Johnson, Crockett	*Harold and the Purple Crayon*
	Harper 1958
Kane, Sharon	*Little Mummy* Golden 1973
Kent, Jack	*The Fat Cat* Parents 1971;
	paper Scholastic 1972
Kent, Jack	*Jack Kent's Book of Nursery Tales*
	Random 1970
Knotts, Howard	*The Winter Cat* Harper 1972
Krasilovsky, Phyllis	*The Cow Who Fell in the Canal*
ill. by Spier, Peter	Doubleday 1957; paper 1972
Lear, Edward	*The Owl and the Pussycat*
ill. by Maxey, Dale	Collins 1969 (UK)
Lenski, Lois	*The Little Family* Doubleday 1932

Author	Title
Lines, Kathleen	*Lavender's Blue* Watts 1954
Macfarlane, Barbara	*Naughty Agapanthus* Nelson 1966
McCloskey, Robert	*Make Way for Ducklings* Viking 1941; paper Penguin 1976
McCloskey, Robert	*Blueberries for Sal* Viking 1948; paper Penguin 1976
Miller, Edna	*Mousekin's ABC* Prentice 1972; paper 1972
Minarik, Else Holmelund ill. by Sendark, Maurice	*A Kiss for Little Bear* Harper 1968
Palmer, Helen	*Fish Out of Water* Random/Beginner 1961
Petersham, Maud and Miska	*The Circus Baby* Macmillan 1950
Prelutsky, Jack ill. by Lobel, Arnold	*The Terrible Tiger* Macmillan 1970; paper 1973
Rose, Elizabeth and Gerald	*How Saint Francis Tamed the Wolf* Harcourt 1959
Sandberg, Inger and Lasse	*Daniel's Mysterious Monster* Black 1973 (UK)
Sandberg, Inger and Lasse	*Daniel and the Coconut Cakes* Black 1973 (UK)
Sendak, Maurice	*In the Night Kitchen* Harper 1970
Sendak, Maurice	*Where the Wild Things Are* Harper 1963
Sutton, Eve and Dodd, Lynley	*My Cat Likes to Hide in Boxes* Parents 1974
Thompson, L.	*At Home* Macmillan 1970 (UK)
Thompson, L.	*Food and Drink* Macmillan 1974 (UK)
Vipont, Elfrida ill. by Briggs, Raymond	*The Elephant and the Bad Baby* Coward 1970
Wood, Joyce ill. by Francis, Frank	*Grandmother Lucy in her Garden* Collins-World 1975

BOOKS MENTIONED IN POSTSCRIPT

Author	*Title*

Grimm, Bros.
  Heins, reteller
  ill. by Hyman, Trina Schart
	Snow White Atlantic-Little 1974

Grimm, Bros.
  Jarrell, Randall, trans.
  ill. by Burkert, Nancy Ekholm
	Snow White and the Seven Dwarfs
	  Farrar 1972

Hoffmann, Felix	*Tom Thumb* Atheneum-McElderry 1973

Watson, Clyde
  ill. by Watson, Wendy
	Tom Fox and the Apple Pie
	  Macmillan 1972

Appendix C

DIAGRAMS TO SHOW CUSHLA'S PARENTS' CHROMOSOME PATTERNS

(Two pairs have been shown, as the chromosomes 'pair off' in the individual.)

Mother's chromosomes: Father's chromosomes:

Possible chromosomatic patterns for child of these parents:

1.   Completely normal, and unable
                                         to transmit abnormality.

2. Identical to father: normal,
    but able to transmit abnormality.

3. Cushla: abnormal and able
    to transmit abnormality.

4. Abnormal: would not become viable
    due to lack of full complement of
    chromosomes.

BIBLIOGRAPHY

BARNEY, David, *Who Gets to Pre-School?* The Availability of Pre-School Education in New Zealand. NZCER (1975) Verry 1975

Britton, James, Editorial note *in* Luria, A. R. and Yudovich, F. I. *Speech and the Development of Mental Processes in the Child.* Penguin (1971)

BROWN, R. and BELLUGI, U., 'Three processes in the child's acquisition of syntax' *in* Endler, S., Boulter, L. R., and Osser, H., *Contemporary Issues in Developmental Psychology.* Holt (1976)

BRUNER, Jerome S., *Studies in Cognitive Growth.* Wiley (1966)

CAZDEN, Courtney B., 'Subcultural differences in child language' *in* Hellmuth, J. (ed.) *The Disadvantaged Child* Vol 2. Brunner-Mazel 1968

GESELL, A., L. *et al.*, *The First Five Years of Life.* Harper (1940)

INHELDER, B., 'Some aspects of Piaget's genetic approach to cognition' *in Society for Research in Child Development Monograph 27 (2)* (1962)

LURIA, A. R. and YUDOVICH, F., *Speech and the Development of Mental Processes in the Child.* Staples (1959)

MERRIAM, Eve, 'How to eat a poem' *in It Doesn't Always Have to Rhyme.* Atheneum (1964)

PIAGET, Jean, *The Child and Reality: Problems of Genetic Psychology.* Penguin 1976 paperback

TOUGH, Joan, *Focus on Meaning: Talking to some purpose with Young Children.* Allen and Unwin (1973)

TURNER, Johanna, *Cognitive Development* Vol C2, *Essential Psychology* Heriot, P. (ed.), Methuen (1975)

VYGOTSKY, L. S., *Thought and Language.* M.I.T. Press (1962)

WATSON, John S., 'Perception of object orientation in infants' *in* Endler, N. S., Boulter, L. R., and Osser, H. *Contemporary Issues in Developmental Psychology.* Holt (1976)

WHITE, Dorothy Neal, *About Books for Children*, NZCER, in conjunction with NZLA (1946)

WHITE, Dorothy Neal, *Books Before Five* NZCER (1954)

ZHUROVA, L. Y., 'The development of analysis of words into their sounds by pre-school children' *in* Fergusson, C. A., and Slobin, D. I. (eds.) *Studies in Child Language and Development.* Holt (1973)

Index

Index

Index

Yeoman family, CUSHLA
  playgroup, 31, 45, 100
  Play Centre, 45, 50, 54, 58, 66, 75, 100-101
  puzzles, 54-55, 71, 75
  reaction to books, 18, 27-29, 33-39, 41, 45-53, 56-57, 60-68, 76-83, 102, Appendix A
  reaction to rhyme, 28, 33, 49, 53, 68-69, 76
  reading to herself, 64, 67-69, 71-72, 76, 105
  Sanchia, relations with, 53, 70, 72, 98, 103, 105
  school, 100-101, 106
  skin condition, 17, 85
  sleeping difficulties, 16, 24-25, 29, 31, 38-39, 55, 84
  speech, *see* language
  Stanford-Binet Intelligence Scale, 83-85
  swimming, 45, 75, 83-84, 100
  toilet training, 45
  traditional stories, 78
  vocabulary, *see* language
  Carol White, compared with, 46-47, 50, 52-53, 56-57, 62-63, 79-80
  writing, 70-72, 104

  extended family, 9, 17, 26-27, 35, 42, 58-60, 73, 82-83, 96-97, 105-107
  Patricia (mother), 15-21, 23-27, 29, 31, 33, 41-43, 45, 49, 53, 57, 60-61, 64-66, 68, 70-74, 76, 79-80, 83-85, 87, 94-104, 107, 109-111, 120
  Sanchia (sister), 40-41, 53, 59-61, 70, 72-74, 80, 82, 98, 105-107
  Stephen (father), 15-21, 23-26, 29, 31, 41-43, 49, 53, 60, 65-66, 70-74, 76, 79, 82-85, 87, 95-104, 107-108, 111, 120
Younghusband Report, 99
YOUNG PUFFIN BOOK OF VERSE, THE, *see* Barbara Ireson
Yudovich, F., 94, 122

Z
Zacharias, Thomas and Wanda, BUT WHERE IS THE GREEN PARROT?, III, 37
Zhurova, L. Y., 34, 123
Zion, Gene, HARRY THE DIRTY DOG, V, 47-48, 51, 56, 64, 111